TERRY DENE: BRITAIN'S FIRST ROCK & ROLL REBEL

DAN WOODING

Edited by Corinna Downes/Joan James
Typeset by Jonathan Downes,
Cover and Layout by SPiderKaT for CFZ Communications
Using Microsoft Word 2000, Microsoft Publisher 2000, Adobe Photoshop CS.

First published in Great Britain by Gonzo Multimedia

c/o Brooks City,
6th Floor New Baltic House
65 Fenchurch Street,
London EC3M 4BE
Fax: +44 (0)191 5121104
Tel: +44 (0) 191 5849144
International Numbers:
Germany: Freephone 08000 825 699
USA: Freephone 18666 747 289

This revised edition © Gonzo Multimedia MMXIII and Dan Wooding

All rights reserved. Without limiting the rights under copyright reserved above, no part of this publication may be reproduced, stored in or introduced into a retrieval system, or transmitted, in any form of by any means (electronic, mechanical, photocopying, recording or otherwise), without the prior written permission of both the copyright owners and the publishers of this book.

ISBN: 978-1-908728-32-6

I would like to dedicate this book to my dear wife, Norma, and my two sons, Andrew and Peter, who have made us very proud. Also to Terry Dene, who is still regarded as the British Elvis of the late 1950s, and recognised as one of the best voices of the British Rock'n'Roll era, as well as his loyal partner, Lucia Liberati, who in recent years has supported him all the along the way. Thanks to all of you!

Some books by Dan Wooding
Junkies are People Too
Stresspoint
I Thought Terry Dene Was Dead
Exit the Devil (with Trevor Dearing)
Train of Terror (with Mini Loman)
Rick Wakeman, the Caped Crusader
King Squealer (with Maurice O'Mahoney)
Farewell Leicester Square (with Henry Hollis)
Uganda Holocaust (with Ray Barnett)
Miracles in Sin City (with Howard Cooper)
God's Smuggler to China (with Brother David and Sara Bruce)
Prophets of Revolution (with Peter Asael Gonzales)
Brother Andrew
Guerilla for Christ (with Salu Daka Ndebele)
Lord, Let Me Give You a Million Dollars (with Duane Logsdon)
Million Dollar Promise (with Duane Logsdon)
Twenty-Six Lead Soldiers
Secret Missions: Stories of Faith in Action (with Brother Andrew)
To Catch the Wind (with Eddie Cairns)
Singing In The Dark (with Barry Taylor)
Lost for Words (with Stuart Mill)
Let There Be Light (with Roger Oakland)
Rock Priest (with David Pierce)
Invitation to the Lion's Den (with David Pierce)
He Intends Victory
Only Believe (with Hannu Haukka)
A Light to India (with Lillian Doerksen)
Blind Faith (with Anne Wooding)
Never say Never: The story of the Rhema Broadcasting Group
From Tabloid to Truth
Treasures Hidden in the Darkness (with Carole Logsdon)
God's Ambassadors in Japan: The Kenny & Lila Joseph Story
Red Dagger
Caped Crusader – Rick Wakeman in the 1970s

Films
Featured in Hollywood on Fire documentary

Foreword by Marty Wilde

Many years ago a young up-and-coming rock 'n' roll singer sat nervously in the darkness of the upper circle at the Finsbury Park Empire, watching the man he considered to be his biggest rival in action. When the show finished, the young rock singer was led backstage and introduced to the star of the show. They nodded courteously, sizing each other up like two prize fighters at the weigh-in, mumbled a few words, and went their separate ways.

I was the up-and-coming rock singer. And the star of the show? Terry Dene.

The next time we met, the roles were drastically reversed. The majority of the British public had discarded the black sheep of rock 'n' roll and, because of his illness, I had to deputise for him at some of his venues and was duly hailed by the boppers of the day as their new rock hero.

Mention Terry today and many of the cynics will smile and reflect on his chequered career, finishing with the classic line "Whatever happened to him?"

Whatever happened to Terry becomes a great deal more comprehensible as you read of the callous way in which he was treated by people who should have known better - many of whom, frankly, will never know better - of the sad little shadows of the past who eased themselves into Terry's life, took everything they could get and, when it

seemed that all was lost, quietly left him .... Dan Wooding's book tells it all.

I felt I wanted to apologise to Terry on behalf of the rest of the human race for the way in which we had treated him over these past years.

We all of us are more or less mixed up, and in one way there are as many answers as there are people with problems (a spell in a psychiatric hospital did more for Terry than the British Army ever could!)

But, speaking as someone who is still searching for the truth, I think that maybe a large helping of good old religion and human kindness might be just the thing that most of us poor lonely souls need ...

God bless you, Terry.

1974

Chapter I

It was one o'clock in the morning and apart from the burly Australian proprietor, Paul Lincoln, the *Two I's* coffee bar in London's Soho was deserted.

His senses reacting with sharp distaste to the atmosphere of stale tobacco smoke and the constrictions of coffee-cup commerce, Lincoln flicked his broom disdainfully at the discarded Pepsi tops and straws littering the floor beneath the plastic-topped tables.

The last pre-selected record dropped onto the turntable and for at least the fiftieth time since Lincoln opened the door to his beat-crazy customers eight hours earlier, Elvis Presley belaboured his decibel-weary ears with a blues lament on life in Heartbreak Hotel.

On the wet pavements outside the *Two I's*, young girls, their skirts two inches below the knee, walked arm in arm with young men whose sideburns reached two inches below the ear. It was November 1956; Elvis and his rocking rivals like Chuck Berry, Fats Domino and Pat Boone were revolutionising the American music scene, but British pop was still in a rut. It was so stereotyped it was a joke. It would have been funny if it hadn't been so pathetic.

The biggest stars were people like Dickie Valentine, Anne Shelton and Joan Regan. Mostly they had come up through dance bands and, once they had established themselves, were apparently safe for life. Nothing seemed to change from year to year. The material they sang – just like its American counterpart – was meaningless and maudlin.

Rock changed everything and almost everyone.

The money monopoly in the music world had gone on for years. The real cash was in sheet music, and the men at the top were the publishers. Broadcasting organisations and disc jockeys were paid to plug their songs and no one could possibly have a hit unless they played ball.

The publishers and, sadly, even the performers, tended to be middle-aged and permanent fixtures, and this meant little joy for the young fans or the young men in the industry. But the end of the plugging system and the birth of rock came about the same time, and the changes began.

In came the young singers and the young hustlers. They saw the wide open music market that their elders were ignoring and smashed the boredom and apathy with their enthusiasm. At last the old stars were threatened by a breed of up-and-coming artists spurred on by youthful, visionary managers.

In fact, the stage was perfectly set for a Terry Dene.

*

Lincoln had just taken a fiver from the till and given it to four young men from Hertfordshire who for three hours had twanged their guitars and swivelled their hips, to the delight of rock-crazy youngsters who identified with the primitive beat by hand-jiving. There was no space for conventional dancing.

The £5 was the group's taxi fare home – and their wages. They did not consider themselves underpaid because every night the *Two I's* brought with it the chance of being discovered. The shy young man who pocketed the £5 was Harry Webb, who had no idea that very soon an agent would ask him to change his name to Cliff Richard.

Lincoln had no way of evaluating Webb's potential, and this disturbed him. Only a short time before, a fair-haired Cockney who sang regularly at the *Two I's* had been whisked away by the shrewd John Kennedy, a New Zealander, given a contract and asked to change his name from Tommy Hicks to Tommy Steele.

Lincoln rubbed half-heartedly at the dried splashes of espresso, filled with annoyance that he was missing out on the discoveries which regularly took place at the *Two I's*. The up-and-coming rock groups were certainly good for business, but while he took 7½p a head for coffee and admission, the smart operators were taking fortune-spinning options on his performers' futures. Lincoln wanted to make big money too – and he knew he could never do it re-filling sugar bowls.

Lincoln was 25 and could be forgiven for not being able to spot the difference between mediocrity and star quality. His background was muscular, rather than musical. He had arrived in London in 1954 to seek fame and fortune as a professional wrestler, after establishing a reputation in the fairground booths back home as the man you couldn't throw out of the ring.

Word soon spread among teenagers that the *Two I's* was the "in" place – and they flocked to listen to would-be pop stars.

It was the birth of a sociological and musical era, and in retrospect the *Two I's* was acclaimed by students of the period as the geographical birthplace of British rock 'n' roll.

As Lincoln cleared away the debris in the early hours of that November day, he acknowledged that the rock revolution had revolutionised his takings, but he was far from satisfied; how could you make a cool million serving ice-cold milk?

He was about to put out the lights when there was a knock at the street-level door. Wearily he climbed the stairs from the basement; through the glass he saw a short rotund figure – Hymie

Zahl, the highly successful West End variety agent.

Lincoln opened the door, led the myopic Zahl down to the basement and produced a bottle of Scotch. He knew that Zahl was not the kind of man to pay purely social calls at that – or any other – time of the day.

"What can I do for you, Mr. Zahl?" he asked. "You haven't come to put money in the juke-box."

"No, but I've come to help put money in your pocket. How come, Paul, that all these people are getting discovered under your nose and you are making nothing out of it? Rock 'n' roll is a licence to print money.

"See if you can't get in first and discover someone yourself. If you can, I'll show you how to make a fortune."

Lincoln knew that for a man with poor eyesight Zahl was no mean visionary and, still smarting from the Tommy Steele affair, he vowed that he would do as Zahl suggested – even if it meant gambling on the unknown.

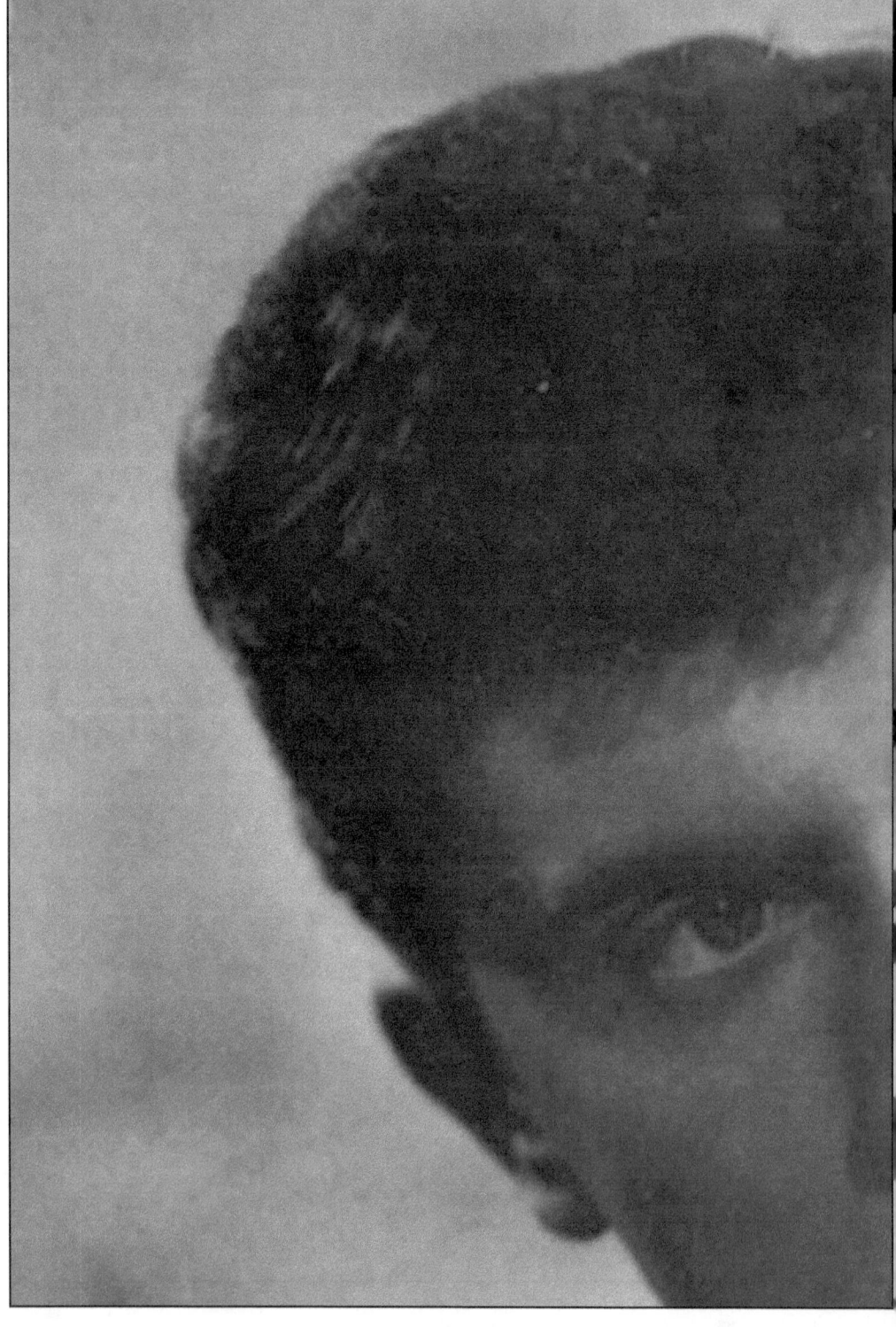

Chapter 2

Christmas 1938 had been a happy one for Mrs. Louise Williams and her husband Albert; five days before, she had given birth to a son. As the baby slept in his cot, the young Cockney couple sat by the fire listening to carols on the radio and discussing what they would call him. It didn't take long, because they agreed about most things. They decided on Terence, and began to plan for the future confidently, if unambitiously; on a machinist's pay, Albert could not afford to be ambitious. One day, of course, they hoped to get a bigger place, a place of their own even, but meanwhile they had each other and the baby, and were happy enough in their little flat above the sweetshop in Lancaster Street, near the Elephant and Castle.

But their happiness was short-lived. Eight months later, the Williams family, together with the rest of London, found themselves facing all the horrors of war: divided families, constant physical and mental strain, air-raids, rationing, uncertainty.

Albert, a former regular soldier, swapped his spanner for a rifle, leaving Mrs. Williams to fend for herself and Terry on his meagre army pay. He wrote regularly, and Louise managed to cope, at least as well as her neighbours.

Until the German bombers increased their raids on the capital to blitz proportions.

As she watched and waited, night after night, knowing the utter helplessness as parachute flares lit the target areas as clearly as daylight, and the sickening certainty of the bomb that would follow, Louise knew that London was no place for a toddler now. All around her, children were being evacuated to the safety of the country; surely Terry should go too? But Mrs. Williams was afraid that Terry, an unusually sensitive child, would be unhappier than most in the care of complete strangers; so in the end she shrugged her shoulders to the danger, and Terry stayed.

One day early in 1943, Mrs. Williams and Terry returned from a shopping expedition – two hours' queuing with coupons for a minute amount of fresh meat – to find that most of the homes in Lancaster Street had been bombed to smithereens. Their own house was untouched, but it was a great shock to see rubble in place of their neighbours' homes.

After that Mrs. Williams, like many other blitz-weary Londoners, became something of a fatalist: if your number was up, there was nothing you could do about it, and there was no point in worrying.

Soon she and Terry moved into Hunter's Buildings, an ugly block of flats near Blackfriars Bridge. The bombing was becoming even more intense, and the air-raid siren never seemed to stop. Two or three times in one night, sometimes, Mrs. Williams would grab Terry from his bed and join the rush for the dank, concrete shelter beneath the block. Often the all-clear would not sound until morning, and they would spend the whole night cooped up with nervy neighbours from the other flats.

It was 8.00 a.m. and Mrs. Williams had slept better than she had for months, in spite of the fact that she had ignored the warden's warning and stayed indoors when the siren had sounded. Anything, she had decided, was preferable to the hours of discomfort in the stale air of the shelter.

But, as she went down to collect the mail, the sound of muffled screaming reached her ears. Horrified, she dashed down to the shelter. She had taken Terry down the previous night and left him with neighbours: now she realised that, when the all-clear had sounded, Terry must have been left behind.

As she unlocked the door and took him in her arms, his whole body shaking from his hour-and-a-half-long nightmare, she vowed she would never let him enter the shelter again; and she never did. Every time the siren went, she would shove Terry's bed under a table in the flat and pray for safety. One night the ceiling collapsed, but neither of them was hurt.

And so mother and son saw out the war – physically, at least, unscathed.

Chapter 3

It didn't take long to mark the register at Friar Street Primary School during the spring term of 1944. Evacuation had cut the intake to a trickle, and the day Terry Williams put in his first appearance the teachers almost outnumbered those to be taught. As far as Terry was concerned, this was a pity ... because he wanted nothing more than to be left alone.

The classroom was dark green and cream and grim, and the other children were tough and boisterous and despised him for his shy, introspective ways.

The teachers made Terry unhappy too. They insisted on trying to make him relate to what they were saying and to what was going on around him and were unremitting in their efforts to penetrate his sad-eyed detachment. They wheedled, cajoled, ridiculed and threatened ... and still the slim fair-haired little boy from the Buildings stared straight ahead over his desk, immersed in thoughts which he did not wish to share.

When the air-raid siren went, Terry was bundled under a big table with his class-mates who, free from the vigilance of the teachers, took the opportunity to punch and kick him as he sat cowering until the emergency passed.

To his teachers, Terry was a problem child and to his class-mates he was a cissy to be bullied during break-time. It was a situation which clearly demanded action and, a few days after his sixth birthday, Mrs. Williams decided to call in a psychiatrist.

"Terry suffers with his nerves like I used to. He's not a bad boy, he just likes to keep his feelings to himself," she explained to the woman.

During the consultations which followed, Terry amply bore out his mother's diagnosis by stubbornly refusing to answer the doctor in anything but monosyllables, despite her painstaking professionalism. On a card which she had to return to the education authority there were blank spaces next to the printed words, "prognosis" and "treatment".

Terry went back to school and, as term succeeded term, life became a little easier. The children continued to persecute him, but only when they could find nothing more interesting to do, and his mentors, frustrated in their failure to make contact, were less abrasive in their attempts to penetrate his personality. However unacceptable he might have been, by the sheer fact of his continued presence he was to some extent accepted.

The flimsy equilibrium was short-lived. When Terry was 11, he was transferred to St. John's and All Saints' Secondary Mixed School in Waterloo Road, Lambeth.

Partly because of long absences from Friar Street due to "nerves" and more usual childhood ailments, his standard of learning was well below average for his age ... and his emotional problems made it virtually impossible for him to make up for lost lesson-time.

In the playground, he entered a new private hell. The girls teased him and the boys bullied him unmercifully, the more so because he rarely responded to their taunts and aggression. Gangs descended upon him like pack-animals determined to eliminate a mutant. One boy who made Terry's nose bleed and left his shirt and self-respect in tatters was asked by a master why he had attacked him.

"Because he's different, sir ... that's why we all do it," was the reply.

Instead of hitting back, Terry used to run around a corner and beat his fists against a wall.

In the evenings, Terry would sometimes go to a youth club to listen to music, which he found helped to soothe away the troubles of the day. He was told always to be home before his father left for work on the night-shift at a South London factory, but one night he had not returned by the time his father left the flat. Next morning a weary Mr. Williams let himself in the front door and saw his son with his back to him.

Without pausing, he launched into a furious tirade. "What did you think you were doing last ..."

As the boy turned round, he stopped speaking and his anger turned to dismay. Terry's lips were swollen and the rest of his face was badly gashed and bruised. He told his father that while he was in the club two older boys from his school had waited for him outside. When he left they jumped on him and beat him up.

Mr. Williams was full of compassion. "But why, son?" he asked gently.

"Because they think I'm different, I suppose."

The Williams tracked down the bullies and started a private prosecution for assault. At the magistrates' court the boys were bound over to keep the peace.

The court case did not bring Terry peace, however: if anything, it made his life even harder. Boys he had never seen before came up to him in the street, hit him and asked: "Is your mum going to take us to court now, Terry?"

The situation became so bad that his mother took to walking with him to the school gates.

Sometimes he broke away from her, sobbing and saying: "I can't go in ... it's no good, I can't go in." Then he would run down the road and spend hours walking in the park. Hounded by his own misery, he would return home jittery and exhausted, often refusing to eat and having nightmares when he went to bed.

After Terry had been at St. John's for a year, his mother took him to see another psychiatrist, who suggested sending him to a remedial boarding school. Mrs. Williams said she would agree if she thought it would do Terry any good, but she didn't – and neither did Terry.

"I want to stay with my mum," he said ... and returned to St. John's and persecution at the hands of his peers.

On the first day of the new school year, in September 1952, Terry found that there was a new boy in his class. At break-time no one talked to him and, as one who permanently felt that school was a strange place, Terry knew how the new boy must feel.

"What's your name?" he asked.

The new boy, despite his big and muscular frame, replied without even a hint of aggression. "Charlie Parker – what's yours?"

Terry told him; then he asked: "Can you fight?"

"A bit, why?"

"They always try it on with new kids here. You want to watch out."

During the next few days "they" duly tried it on and Charlie was involved in two fights. To Terry's delight he won both – and the grudging respect of every boy in the school.

Terry and Charlie became firm friends. Although Terry's quasi-cultured accent stood out like a beacon in a sea of Cockney and this, together with an interest in current affairs earned him the nickname of "The Professor", the other boys no longer picked on him with the malevolence of earlier days. Terry was accepted once more ... Charlie saw to that. Gradually his work improved, his confidence increased and his stunted personality began to develop. Masters were impressed by his thirst for knowledge; he won a place in the school football team; he became the regular soloist in the school choir and, with Charlie, joined the drama class.

Charlie, now production manager for a Lambeth brewery and married with a family, recalled: "When the drama class first started we were made to act out an animal. I got all embarrassed, but when Terry was told to be a monkey, he was terrific. He really got into the part ... he loved appearing in front of people. He loved acting and for a long time he wanted to be an actor, but he said that when you're just the boy from the Buildings you might as well forget it – it just doesn't happen.

"Terry hated violence. He didn't have more than a couple of scraps. He would take so much and then everything would explode in his head and there was no stopping him, but that didn't happen very often.

"He didn't mix with the others too well. The lads seemed interested in chatting up the girls. He was more interested in learning. The area didn't really suit Terry. He was a very sensitive, emotional person and he was out of his element with the boys. He even spoke different."

Terry and Charlie became interested in astronomy. With adolescent zeal they pored over books on the subject at the public library and talked about buying a telescope and setting up their own observatory. When the boys teased Terry about his stargazing he was completely undisturbed and predicted a lunar landing. One youth was so shaken by the prediction that he felt moved to stop Mrs. Williams on the street. He told her: "Your Terry's loopy – he thinks men are going to land on the moon!" And Terry's nickname was changed to "Moon Man."

The Williams' flat in Hunter's Buildings was so cramped that Terry slept permanently on a camp bed in the living room, but despite the lack of space, one item of furniture was sacred – an English upright piano.

That piano probably saved Terry's sanity.

Mrs. Williams was an untrained but fairly able pianist and many of her family played musical instruments, so she was not in the least surprised when her son eyed the ivories with interest at an early age.

Before he met Charlie, in the days when he felt the whole world was against him, he used to sit for hours at the keyboard soothing away his troubles with his own interpretations of tunes he had heard on the radio. By the time he was 14, his natural ear for music had developed to the extent that he could reproduce almost any melody from memory.

In the evenings Charlie sat listening to him, enthralled. "He was brilliant," he recalled. "He couldn't read music but his memory for tunes was amazing and he played so movingly that sometimes it brought tears to my eyes."

Terry didn't cry, however. His crying days were over ... or at least he thought they were.

Chapter 4

"You're a nothing, Williams. You're a little squirt. You shouldn't be allowed to live."

The words were frighteningly familiar. Only the time and the place had changed.

Terry's early school days should have taught him about bullies, but now, at work, he was being examined on what he had learnt – and he didn't know the answer.

This time the words came from a man at the Oxford Street firm where Terry had been given a job as a bicycle messenger.

"Why does this guy keep picking on me?" he moaned to Charlie Parker. "I can't take much more of it."

Terry boiled with suppressed rage. He longed to take a swing at his burly tormentor, but knew he would come off worse if he did.

"Charlie, what can I do, mate? He's making my life hell."

Charlie, like Terry, had left school and was gingerly charting a path through adolescence. The pair agreed that their last year at school had been their best. They knew their way round and the other kids showed a certain respect, mainly because they were older.

But now they had left, and were at the bottom again. Everyone was older, more experienced. Going to work was rather like going to school again for the first time, and in Terry's case there was another sinister parallel – he was being bullied once more.

"The only way you'll get this bloke's respect is to hit him," said Charlie. "You might get hurt, but I reckon it'll do the trick."

"OK! If you say so, I'll do it."

Brave words. Terry hardly slept that night, wondering if he would be able to summon up enough courage to carry his plan through. Next morning he curtly refused his cornflakes and tea, kissed his mum good-bye, donned his cycle clips and headed for Oxford Street – and trouble. By the time he got to the Oval cricket ground he had made up his mind that nothing would stop him. He was going to bowl this bully over with a right hook – and then run for his life!

"Late again, Williams!" yelled his tormentor as Terry leaned his bike against the car park wall. "I don't know why we pay you wages, you're just a liability ..."

Terry needed no more prompting. He let fly with a hook that Randolph Turpin would have been proud of. It landed smack on the man's chin and sent him sprawling. A big grin spread over Terry's face. "That'll teach you to pick on me!" he yelled down at the fallen figure.

But the grin soon faded as the man heaved himself up and charged like an angry bull. Terry scarpered, but not quickly enough, and the incensed man grabbed his prey and started to make amends. Terry went dizzy with the beating, but suddenly the blows ceased and through the haze he saw his rival hopping up and down holding his right hand. He had knocked out part of one of Terry's front teeth and it had become embedded in his hand.

An ambulance was called and the injured bully was taken to hospital to have the tooth extracted from his blood-covered hand.

"You ... Williams!" he shouted as he was helped away. "I'll get you when I get back."

"Serves you right," Terry yelled from a safe distance as the ambulance doors slammed. "I should have hit you a long time ago!"

With the famous victory under his belt, the new middle-weight champion of Oxford Street jauntily collected some messages and headed for the nearby offices. He whistled loudly as he entered the foyer of a large store.

"You all right, son?" asked a concerned commissionaire. "You look like you've been in a fight."

"I have been in a fight," winked Terry, "and I took the title!"

Terry couldn't wait to leave work that night. He wanted to tell Charlie the whole gory but triumphant tale. His evening meal dried up in the oven as he went to the Parkers' flat, and as his friend opened the door, wiping the remnants of his sausage, egg and chips from his lips, Terry's grin showed a wide, bloody gap between his teeth. "I've done it," he said. "I've clobbered him good and proper, just like you said."

"You look as if you've been clobbered yourself," replied his mystified mate.

"Well, he went to hospital, didn't he? And I didn't – so I must have won!"

A new Terry was born and over the next few months he gained in confidence. At last he felt he could hold his head high and solve at least some of his problems with his fists. He was no longer scared of bullies – after all, hadn't he just put one in his place?

Soon after the punch-up, Terry decided it would help Charlie if he joined him at the clock maker's and repairers in Southwark where he worked. If Terry was close at hand, perhaps he could protect Charlie if he met with trouble.

The deathly silence of the firm was broken up by the steady tick-tock of time-pieces as they came alive, created or mended by men without smiles.

They were dedicated men who hadn't time for laughter and music during the working day, and Terry was quickly ticked off by a foreman for singing loudly. At sixteen, he knew the hit tunes of Johnnie Ray and Frankie Laine by heart, and he made sure the middle-aged clock men did too.

One day an irate foreman couldn't stand it any longer. "Why don't you belt up? Can't you see we're trying to work?" he shouted.

"Keep your hair on," Terry yelled back, trying to control his temper. He rushed into a dingy back yard to try to cool off and beat his fists against the palm of his sweaty hand.

"Terry, come back in," called Charlie. So he did, and the foreman demanded to know where he had been.

"Outside -- to cool off."

"You can cool for good. Here are your cards," said the angry foreman.

So Terry was out of work again.

He drifted from job to job with little enthusiasm. He was a timber "hunker" in a factory, a trainee draughtsman and a plumber's mate. Then Charlie decided to join a gang of Teddy boys, leaving Terry to fend for himself. It was a blow, for he thought their friendship would go on unchecked for ever. The break brought intense misery for him: Charlie was the friend with whom he had shared his innermost secrets, ambitions and fears. Now Charlie didn't want to know him.

"I used to go home from work every night and have my supper. Then I would sit around with my mum," Terry recalled. "On Wednesdays I would visit an aunt and on Saturdays and Sundays it was the pictures with my parents."

Fortunately, Charlie's gang days were short-lived and soon the teenaged pals were re-united. Terry perked up; so did his luck, for he got a job as a packer at a busy record shop in Oxford Street, for which he was paid the princely sum of £3.50 a week.

Rock 'n' roll was beginning to capture the imagination of the country, and young Terry was one of the first converts; as he checked off records against order lists and then carefully packed them into containers, Terry hummed Elvis Presley hits. He sang the songs against the roar of the traffic as he cycled home, and, as he settled into his camp bed in the living room of the flat at Hunter's Buildings, he dreamed dreams of the King of Rock. He studied pictures of Elvis, he listened to Elvis discs and copied down all the words he could catch. When his mum and dad were out, he would stand in front of a mirror with a Presley record playing at top volume and mime to it, every hip-swinging gesture thrown in.

At the record shop he discovered Dave, a drummer who shared his enthusiasm for Elvis, and they would get together at nights to rehearse the songs of their leader.

At Christmas 1956, Terry decided it was time for him to be discovered. The record company he worked for was holding its Christmas party and all the executives were coming to enjoy the freely flowing booze and politely applaud the staff as they stumbled through their party pieces.

Terry left the shop early to prepare for his big night. He was going to show the bosses he could sing every bit as well as Elvis and ought to be signed up. Nights of rehearsal with Dave were going to pay off.

He stopped off at a hardware store to buy some brown paint and a brush. These would give him sideburns, which nature hadn't yet provided. His hand trembled as he paused in front of the bathroom mirror to paint on the "Elvis" trademark. As the paint dried, he carefully combed his hair the way Presley had his, and went over the words of "Poor Boy" for the umpteenth time that week.

His heart pounded as he stood in the wings of the improvised stage watching one of the middle-aged record assistants trying, not very successfully, to put over a Max Miller act. The record chiefs squirmed with embarrassment, and compensated themselves with whisky on the rocks.

"Now, I want to introduce you to a young man who will one day sweep Oxford Street – with a broom, Ha! Ha!" said the bright MC. "No, I'm only joking, ladies and gentlemen, I want you to give a big hand to young Terry Williams, who tells me he wants to stop packing records and start making 'em."

Terry rushed on stage clutching his guitar, and with a mixed-up Cockney-mid-Atlantic accent, a sultry look, and a fascinating quiff bouncing from eye to lazy, heavy-lidded eye, thanked his disinterested audience for "that tremendous ovation". Then he launched into "Poor Boy" followed in quick succession by "Hound Dog" and "Blue Suede Shoes", as Dave bashed away on his drums.

"I reckon we are the poor boys having to listen to this nonsense," murmured a cigar-smoking executive, downing another compensatory drink.

Two more songs were breathlessly pounded out to the intoxicated audience, and then Terry took the hint, acknowledged the unenthusiastic applause from his audience and slunk off.

It was back to record-packing after Christmas. There was obviously going to be no record contract for the boy from the Buildings; not from this disc company, at least.

Then Terry met Margaret, an attractive girl who recognised his talent and introduced him to Rory Blackwell, the leader of a rock band. Margaret soon disappeared from Terry's life, but later married another of rock's stormy characters, Gene Vincent, a tragic singer who had two fast hits – "Be Bop a Lula" and "Blue Jean Bop" – and then endured repeated breakdowns and failed comebacks before his untimely death.

Blackwell arranged an audition, with the promise of a job with the band. Out came the brown paint and on went the sideboards again.

"I'll give you twenty-five bob a night, Terry; how does that grab you?"

"Great, Rory. Wait till I tell my mum – she'll be tickled pink!"

So Terry left his record-packing job to concentrate on packing them in at the band's dates. He soon made his first record – a "demo" disc – and sent it to a top record producer. It came back, with a message: "Come back in 10 years when you can sing!"

The first week singing with Rory's band in the pubs around London was exciting for Terry. The band rehearsed during the day and then a keyed-up Terry stepped on stage and swivelled his hips in the smoke-filled bars, to give his everything.

But a new job brought a new problem.

"Have a drink, boy," the customers would say after the spot. "Have another, son. Go on, it won't do you no harm!"

Terry soon became a minor celebrity and was loving it.

"Great show, Terry boy; have a drink, what would you like? Whisky neat?"

Six nights a week, Terry was singing and getting tanked up on free booze. Whisky, mainly, flowed freely and night after night a befuddled Terry Williams would stagger on stage and slur through the Elvis repertoire.

"That kid's stoned out of his mind," a pub manager complained to Rory one night. "Don't bother to play here again."

"Look, Terry, lay off the drink. You can't take it," Rory would warn.

"Don't tell me how to live my life," the up-and-coming celebrity retorted. "Just because you pay me twenty-five bob a night, that doesn't mean you own me."

Despite his heavy drinking, Terry would make the star-struck girl customers scream as he went through his act. The male customers would squirm.

"You're just a pouf, kid," one tough-looking boy told Terry as he left the stage one night.

The girl on his arm told him to shut up, but he wouldn't. "You're a pouf. Singer boy, I'm talking to you!"

Terry, well tanked-up, stopped. "I'll show you what sort of pouf I am, mate – take that!"

He landed a hefty swing on the youth's jaw, sending him flying across the pub. The boy came back at Terry only to be sent sprawling back again across the bar. Nursing a sore head, he grabbed his girl: "Let's go, Mavis. I won't come here again!"

Night after night there was trouble. His schoolmates would never have recognised this raging animal prepared to take on anyone who stood in his way. Fights, drunkenness ... it couldn't go on. Rory was getting fed up with his temperamental star turn.

"Take a few days' rest, Terry. Maybe that will sort out your trouble," Rory told him.

He took a short rest. The first night back he took another customer on, and was fired.

"That's it, Terry. You've got talent, no doubt about that, but you spoil yourself with this behaviour," Rory told him.

Not really upset, Terry headed for Soho and the *Two I's* coffee bar where he occasionally dropped in for a coffee. He hadn't been during his time with Rory, but he had heard that things were really happening there. Mr. Lincoln, my name's Terry Williams," he said as the brawny ex-wrestler took his admission money. "Can I have a go at singing tonight?"

"OK, lad. But take your turn in the queue. Stick to the rota."

In the month since Hymie Zhal's visit, Lincoln had taken a new interest in the pimply, enthusiastic cabaret performers. He liked the look of Terry, and stopped serving coffee as he walked on to the tiny stage with his guitar and began singing. When he finished he received an ecstatic ovation. Lincoln signalled him over. "Look, can you come down here again on Friday? I might be able to get someone to hear you. He's a West End agent."

"Can I? Can bats fly?" replied Terry. "I'll be there, Mr. Lincoln; I won't let you down."

As Terry settled round a table with a group of teenagers to watch other potential rockers go through their noisy paces, Lincoln made his way to a phone to call Zahl.

"Sorry to phone you at this time of night, Mr. Zahl, but I think I've found the boy we want. He's been here tonight and he looks like a winner."

"You can make it Friday night? Great!"

Lincoln settled back behind the counter, humming to himself; was Terry's the face that would make him a fortune?

Chapter 5

Hundreds of unblinking eyes, painted on the walls by customers, stared at Terry as he sat in the rather bizarre atmosphere of the *Two I's*. It was four days before his meeting with the agent and he could think of nothing but the big day.

With him around the coffee-stained table were two mates, Mickie and Alex.

Later, Mickie Most became the millionaire boss of a record label, a walking hit machine who cut discs for Donovan, *The Animals*, *Herman's Hermits*, Lulu, *The Yardbirds*, Jeff Beck and Suzi Quatro, to name but a few. In those days, he was just another 17-year-old kid from south of the river, but his eye for an opening was already sharp.

He had heard that Otto Preminger was paying film extras £3.50 a day at Shepperton Studios, where he was making *Joan of Arc*.

"Look, lads, we're all broke. It could be a giggle," said Mickie. "All we've got to do is rake up the train fare from Waterloo, and I reckon some of the kids here will be good for a touch. It'll take your mind off Friday, Terry. What do you think?"

Terry smiled. "I might get discovered again and become a film star!"

Mickie scraped the money together and they set off for Waterloo, where they spent the night in a chilly waiting room with down-and-outs so they could catch the first train in the morning.

The money didn't stretch to food, so when the train pulled into Shepperton Station they were not only tired, but ravenously hungry.

Most, always a good organiser, appointed Alex, later his partner in the Most Brothers group, as official bread gatherer and Terry milk bottle snatcher. Terry and Mickie chatted amiably with a baker, asking him the way to the studios, while Alex swooped and collected an armful of loaves.

They greedily ripped large chunks out of the warm bread and, as they fled down the street with an angry baker waving his arms behind them, Terry grabbed three bottles of milk for an instant breakfast.

When the dishevelled trio arrived at the imposing studio, Mickie acted as spokesman.

"We believe you want extras for *Joan of Arc*. We are very experienced at this sort of thing."

The man on the gate didn't seem convinced but let them through, and soon the budding movie stars were transformed into peasants for a crowd scene.

"Look you two, I'm so tired I don't think I could face a day's work," said Terry with a long, deliberate yawn. "I think I'll have a sleep in that shed over there. Nobody will miss me. Coming?"

The others agreed and all three got their heads down in the shed. Soon loud snores echoed around the set.

But yells and cries of "She's burning! She's burning!" from panic-stricken technicians woke them up.

Sleepily they went to see what was happening and spotted Jean Seberg as Joan of Arc, chained to a great stake. A huge pile of wood around her was blazing and crackling and her hair was singeing and about to catch fire.

"Cor, that's realistic," said Terry.

"It isn't meant to be that realistic," said Mickie. "Her hair isn't supposed to catch fire!"

The film crew fought like mad to free her from the stake, and damp down her blazing hair, but the excitement was soon over and the sleepy three took advantage of the confusion to go back to "bed" again. This time it was not for long – they were discovered and dragged, protesting, on to the set to join hordes of other extras including many others from the *Two I's*, after easy money.

"I want you to shout 'Burn the witch, burn the witch' when I say so," They were told by a man with a megaphone.

But the *Two I's* entourage didn't co-operate, and instead screamed slogans like "Elvis forever," and "Long live rock 'n' roll."

Mickie Most told me later: "Otto Preminger was going crazy. Not surprising, really, because we were ruining his film!"

When Terry, Mickie and Alex finished their day's "filming" they joined the pay queue, but the accountant didn't want to know.

"You're not getting any money from me," he said firmly. "You lot have caused more trouble than anybody. I reckon you ought to pay us."

A prolonged row went on and a long queue of other extras who wanted to get off home had to wait.

Finally, the money man gave in and paid the three – but only on condition they never came back.

The trio headed for the nearest fish and chip shop and stuffed themselves with as much food as they could take, which by then was a lot.

The next day, Wednesday, was spent rehearsing in a Circle Line carriage on the Underground. Most of the time the carriage was empty except for the three rocking occupants, but when an unfortunate passenger did climb in, they would pass the hat round. The passenger usually thought they were buskers, coughed up a few coppers and climbed out at the next station!

Terry thought Friday would never come. He tossed and turned all through Thursday night, and woke up with a churning feeling inside. What if he fluffed this chance? What if the agent didn't come? Doubts flooded his mind.

He got to the *Two I's* early and was warmly greeted by Lincoln. "You needn't pay tonight, Terry," he said generously. "Mr. Zahl, the agent, should be here about eight o'clock and then you can do your piece. Don't look so worried. He won't eat you."

Terry spotted Zahl as he lumbered into the coffee-bar, puffing an expensive cigar, peering through his thick glasses and the smoke.

Lincoln called a singer off the tiny stage, and helped Terry up. "Go on, then," he said. "Do your stuff."

The spotlight picked out Terry's tiny figure as he swung his hips into action and jerked his way through an Elvis impression. It went down well with the hand-jiving customers.

Just one number was enough to convince the dead-pan Zahl that this was the boy to make him and Lincoln a mint of money. He lumbered over to Terry and said: "Come across the road to the pub, boy. I want to talk to you."

Terry ordered a shandy as Zahl took out a sheaf of crisp fivers. "That's real money, son, the sort you'll be earning soon. What do you think about that?"

"Sounds great. I'll be able to buy a new guitar and some more records."

"Sure, boy," said Zahl, slapping Terry on the shoulder. "Me and Mr. Lincoln are going to make a star out of you. We're going to fix your hair and teeth, and soon we'll have your name in lights!"

Chapter 6

"Terry Williams just isn't a commercial name," said Hymie as he entertained Lincoln in his plush West End Office. "It's got to go. If our mean and moody boy is going to attract the fans, he must have a name that hits home."

Lincoln agreed. Back in his coffee-bar he asked a roundtable customers' conference for their advice.

"I reckon it should be Terry Willis," someone said.

"You must be joking," declared Mickie Most, as he downed his Pepsi. "I can see it now – Terry Wills and the Woodbines. You'd be the laughing stock of Tin Pan Alley. Mind you, a few smokers might buy your records!"

"How about Clint Lust and the Fleshpots," sarcastically suggested another customer.

"Get lost," lashed Terry, annoyed that anyone could joke about such an important subject.

Not surprisingly, it was Most who came up with the best suggestion. "I've got it – Terry Dean. There's a cult going on now about James Dean, that actor who got killed in a car crash a couple of years ago. Yes, it's got to be Terry Dean."

"What about the spelling, Mickie? Don't you think it should be changed?" queried Terry. Mickie thought for a second: "O.K. Make it D.E.N.E."

Terry was pleased. "That's the same spelling as *Dene's Holiday Camp* where my mum and dad used to take me on holiday. I can say I took the name because of the nice holidays we had there."

So, in the noisy excitement of the *Two I's* coffee-bar, Terry Williams lost his identity and became Terry Dene, Britain's first hell-raising pop star.

"You'll need lots of time to rehearse, so it's the Circle Line for you again, Terry," said Most, keen to promote his friend's career. "I'll make sure he knuckles down to it in the carriages,

Paul."

And while Hymie and Paul attempted to sell Terry Dene to bookers, Mickie kept him hard at it in the unlikely atmosphere of the swaying carriages, which were without a doubt the cheapest rehearsal rooms in London. One ticket sufficed for the day, and they were crowded with budding stars like Adam Faith, Lionel Bart, and Wally Whyton, all hopefully strumming their way to the top.

Hymie managed to assemble a backing group for Terry, and called them the *Dene-aces*. The group comprised Terry Kennedy (lead guitar), Mickey McDonough (rhythm guitar), Ron Prentice (bass guitar) and Clem Cattini (drums). A van was bought and their name was painted gaudily on each side. At the back was the slogan: "YOU ARE FOLLOWING TERRY DENE AND THE DENE-ACES."

Slowly, very slowly, bookings trickled in, and Terry Dene was in business, albeit not as yet very profitable business. The biggest audience during his first few professional appearances was 40. Then Hymie got a booking for a Sunday night concert at Romford, Essex, which attracted a more promising audience – 200.

"Terry, my boy, you are doing quite well," said Hymie as he tucked into lunch shortly after. "But how would you really like to hit the big time? Paul and I have fixed it for you to sing in front of 4,000 people at the Royal Albert Hall on Saturday."

"You're joking, Hymie," said Terry, his jaw dropping.

"My life! Would I joke with you? Paul knows the promoter of the wrestling show in which the Welterweight Championship of the World is being staged. He says it's all right for you to sing in the ring during the interval.

"It's the first time a rock 'n' roll singer has ever performed in a wrestling ring, so don't mess it up. We're counting on you."

Terry lost count of the times he left his dressing room at the Victorian auditorium for the men's toilet. His nerves were taut and his inside rolled around. He didn't know if he would have the courage to go head. He paced the dressing-room like a caged tiger. He coughed, scratched and coughed again.

"Time to go, Terry," said Paul, walking into the room as his ashen-faced singer made a last check in the mirror of his striking outfit of blue shirt with yellow collar and blue jeans.

"Don't forget, we're all depending on you. Good luck."

Terry tightened the laces of his rather inappropriate grey suede shoes, cleared his dry throat, crossed his shaking fingers, and headed out into the massive arena with an equally nervous group. The fans jeered and booed as he climbed into the ring and kept it up as he launched into his first song, "Blue Suede Shoes". Peanuts and cakes came hurtling into the ring, but he continued bravely.

"Keep going, boy, you're doing well," yelled Hymie as Terry looked for a moment as if he was going to make a run for it. "You've really knocked them out!"

As he spoke, a bag of peanuts hit Terry square on his sweating, powdered forehead and nearly knocked *him* out, such was the venom with which it was thrown. But during his next number, "Poor Boy", the fans warmed to the slight 18-year-old contorting in the spotlight, and many began cheering. By the time he had finished his historic four-number "gig", Terry Dene had wrested the hard hearts of 5,000 fans – and, more important, of Jack Good, producer of television's first pop show, "Six-Five Special", who had been invited along by Paul Lincoln. Good has been hailed as pop's first intellectual, and realised that pop was clearly a major phenomenon, not just a craze which would quickly pass, as others then thought. He quickly recognised that Dene had talent and immediately booked him for his show. His judgement proved right; after Terry's first appearance, the B.B.C. had 500 letters asking about him. The fans didn't know, however, that Terry had been up all night after swallowing a fistful of pep pills. But the pills pepped up his performance. They offered a giddy sense of well-being that could temporarily surmount his nerves.

Things moved so quickly for young Terry after this television appearance that he was still breathless when Hymie dragged him along to Dick Rowe, one of Decca's top record producers.

"This is the boy I was telling you about, Dick," said Hymie, lighting up the inevitable cigar. "I'm giving you a big break by bringing him to you first."

Rowe had seen Terry's first appearance on *Six-Five Special* and realised he could be a big star, but he knew he needed to point out Terry's weaknesses to him.

"Terry, who is your favourite singer?"

"It's Elvis, Mr. Rowe. I listen to his records for hours at home. I try to copy his style. I think he's the greatest."

Rowe sat back in his swivel chair. "I don't mean to be hard, Terry, but that's your problem. You're just a second-rate Elvis. I don't think the kids of this country will be satisfied with a handy carbon copy, they want an original singer."

Terry was taken aback. "I don't copy Elvis in everything," he countered. "I try and ..."

"Look, if you want to make hit records, listen to what I say, and do what I say. If you don't you might as well pack up now. O.K.?"

Terry thought for a minute and then nodded. Rowe suggested "A White Sport Coat" as his first record. It was written by Marty Robbins, the American singer-composer.

"Terry, this is a record of the song. I want you to take it home and learn it," said Rowe. Terry must have learned it well because on the fifth take in the studio, the record was "in the can" – just as he sang it. The man at the heavy console gave the thumbs-up sign to Rowe, who grinned with satisfaction.

"A White Sport Coat" was a raving success. It shot into the Top Twenty, and beat the sales of Marty Robbins' original version. It spun relentlessly on café jukeboxes, housewives hummed it as they "Hoovered" the carpet, and men on production lines at factories whistled its catchy tune all day long. Radio Luxemburg disc jockeys beamed it each night over the airwaves to Britain. Hymie decided Terry's gimmick should be a white sport coat and a pink carnation, and kitted him out accordingly.

Lincoln was not very keen on the idea and says that in retrospect it was a mistake. "I never spoke my mind in those days because I felt Hymie knew the music business better than me. I would have preferred Terry to have had an evil image like Gene Vincent, who used to dress all in black leather.

"To further the bad-boy image, I would have taken him to a club where he could have hit someone and punched a few journalists; that would have been nearer to what Terry Dene really became like in those days."

The white sport coat was the main gimmick of their singer. He was such a rave that they didn't have to resort to others, like planting girls in the audiences to scream every time he moved. And they didn't provide Terry with suits which came to bits when fans started tugging, another popular trick. But they did launch a fan club and coined a term which swept through the country like wildfire. Thousands of teenagers proudly wore badges declaring: "I'm a Dene-ager". They were fed with reams of inane information about their idol in a stream of newsletters, and the Press soon latched on to the new Dene-age sensation, who, as one paper declared, "Out-Steeles Tommy".

He was the rage of the disc-buying youngsters: Britain's answer to Elvis Presley.

"The first time the £4-a-week Cockney Sparrow went into a recording studio," confided the *Daily Sketch*, "he wore his blue serge suit, a well-scrubbed face and mum's words next to his heart: 'You can only do your best, son. And mind you say "sir" and don't give any lip.'

"That was three months ago. He is now earning £100 a week, but he is still wearing the same suit and face, and mum's advice is his sheet-anchor.

"TERRY DENE is his name. But in the Buildings at the Elephant and Castle, he's 'The Sparrer'."

So Terry had finally made it. His personal reward was a bigger and better collection of the Pelvis's discs and an occasional word of praise from Hymie and Paul. Mum and Dad were proud of their boy. He'd shown everyone who once laughed at him that the laugh was on them. The nervous kid was now a confident, polished and popular performer.

Chapter 7

Not only was Terry Dene a riot; he created them wherever he went. Whatever the date, in television studio or theatre, the girls turned out in their thousands.

Soon he was forced to become a minor master of disguise to escape the clutches of hysterical crowds. Sometimes he was a "tramp", drifting through a back door as his group dashed out of the stage door. Other times he wore large hats and ill-fitting overcoats. He often fooled the fans, but when they recognised him he had to race for his life. Like the time when he had finished another rocking encore at the Dublin theatre where he was booked for a week, and was on his way to his dressing room. Weary stewards had fought for 40 minutes to prevent love-struck girls from getting on stage. Like soldiers in the First World War, they attacked in waves – down the aisles. One girl managed to evade the strong-arm men and dived across the orchestra pit and on to the stage.

She rushed at Terry, who calmly put his arm round her and finished his song "C'mon and be loved", kissed her gently on the cheek, and pointed her in the direction of the wings.

"You'll have to leave in disguise tonight, Mr. Dene," said the theatre manager as the chanting of "We want Terry" got more and more frenzied outside the theatre. "I have this old trilby and mac in the props box which should fit you. Try them on."

Terry sat in front of his dressing-room mirror, peppered with electric lights, wiping the last of the thick make-up from his face. He still hadn't absorbed the happenings of the last few weeks. People no longer treated him as a sick joke: now they queued for hours to catch even a glimpse of him. He was topping the bill across the nation. It was now "Mr. Dene", not plain Williams.

He was a celebrity. He went into hotels through the front door and commissionaires, who would once have rasped: "Get lost, sonny" were now treating him as a VIP.

"O.K., Terry," shouted Clem Cattini, the Dene-aces drummer, above the chanting. "We'll go out the stage door and then you leave by the side door. Hope you make it. If you don't, it's been nice knowing you ..."

TERRY DENE: BRITAIN'S FIRST ROCK AND ROLL REBEL

The crowds surged forward as the Dene-aces emerged and, despite a score of policemen with linked arms, were, for a time, pinned against the stage door. "Where's Terry?" shouted a distraught fan. "He's not with them. He's got away!"

Terry slid slowly away from the theatre, his battered trilby pulled tight over his head, his hands in his pockets, congratulating himself that he had escaped to safety. But then a girl spotted him.

"That's him! I'm sure it is. He's dressed up so we wouldn't know it was him."

The hunt was on. Terry, the fox, was quickly away. He tore off the restricting overcoat and his trilby blew away and settled in the gutter, where it was trampled by several hundred fans chasing their quarry.

Terry knew they meant business and breathlessly scampered for his life, dodging into a side street in the hope they would lose the scent.

But the girls were now just 50 yards behind, so he doubled back on the main road into a cul-de-sac, dived into a fish and chip bar, slammed the door and, with a hint of terror in his voice, asked a white-coated man frying cod and chips, "Can I hide behind your counter? It's very important."

"Help yourself," replied the mystified fish-fryer. Then, looking behind Terry, he saw an amazing sight. The shop window was beginning to bow under the pressure of the crowds outside!

"Look, what have you done? You haven't killed someone have you?"

"No. I'm a rock singer. Those girls are after me."

Just then, two red-faced cops who had overtaken the fans opened the door. "Where is he?" they asked anxiously.

"I'm here," said Terry, popping his head above the counter.

"O.K. Mr. Dene. You come with us; we'll get you home safely."

"You sure?" he said hesitantly, eyeing the whites of hundreds of feminine eyes.

The big Irish cops grabbed him by the arms and rushed him out into the road. "Make way, please," an officer shouted. And they did. Terry was hustled the quarter of a mile to his O'Connell Street hotel, with chanting, screaming girls just a few paces behind.

Police formed a semi-circle around the foyer as Terry ran up to his room. He slumped on his bed, shut his eyes and tried to relax. It wasn't easy, because outside the chanting of "We want Terry ..." reverberated again and again.

The noise went on for 15 minutes, until there was a knock on his door and a policeman entered.

"Look, Mr. Dene, these girls are blocking the street. We can't get traffic through and the whole thing is getting out of hand. They say they are going to stay all night."

"Please go out and sing for them. Just one song will do the trick, I'm sure it will."

So Terry grabbed a spare guitar, opened his window and went on to the balcony. As he emerged, the centre of Dublin erupted. Terry lifted his hand and the fans responded with quiet.

"I'm going to sing one number and then I want you all to go home quietly," he shouted.

It was the perfect choice. Ears strained as he sang "When Irish Eyes are Smiling". As he finished, they clapped, cheered – and then dispersed. Police heaved a sigh of relief and Terry went to bed.

*

The week in Dublin was his first "overseas" experience. It was added to by the thrill of flying.

The exuberant group was chatting in the aircraft heading back to London when a quiet-spoken American asked if he could join them.

"Well, what do you do?" he asked Terry.

Terry told him, pleased at the man's interest. The American bombarded the rock and rollers with questions, never pausing to tell them about his "business".

As they left the plane, a steward stopped Terry and asked "Did you know who you were talking to?"

"No," said Terry. "I'm afraid I didn't."

"That was Walt Disney ..."

*

At the time, Terry's number one fan, comedian Jimmy Tarbuck, soon became like a brother. They first met while Terry was playing the Liverpool Empire, and a girl fan persuaded him to visit Jimmy's home and say hello to his mum.

"I was thrilled when he came round," said Tarbuck. "He was then a big, big star and I was still doing the round of the local contests. We hit it off straight away, and my mum loved him!"

"She ran theatrical digs and he moved in for the rest of the week."

Jimmy returned to the Empire with Terry that night and was there, "taking in the atmosphere", each night for the rest of the week.

They soon became like brothers in more ways than one. "I joined him on his tours for several days at a time," Jimmy recalled. "I did any job Terry required, I was like his valet, doing his shirts and that sort of thing.

"It was during one of the tours I became 'Jimmy Dene'. I left Terry's dressing room one night to find screaming girls chanting 'We want Terry, we want Terry'. I told them he was busy and couldn't come out.

"One girl asked me 'Who are you?' I told her I was Terry's brother.

"She replied. 'You'll do', and so the girls queued up for the prized signature of 'Jimmy Dene'. From then on I posed as Terry Dene's brother and signed accordingly wherever we went. It was quite a scream."

Jimmy later became compere for shows on which Terry appeared, and later the incredible rock 'n' roll package shows. Soon he was a star himself.

He still has a great affection for his "brother" and feels he learned a lot during this time.

"They were very happy days," he told me. "Terry was a great lad. I thought the world of him. Unfortunately, he later became rather like George Best is today, and his troubles were widely publicised."

Among the hordes of screaming girls in the Liverpool Empire during Terry's week-long run was 15-year-old Joyce Baker from Huyton.

"I worshipped Terry and screamed with the rest when he sang," Joyce told me. "A short time after this I became a big fan of Terry's rival, Marty Wilde. I was one of his biggest fans ..."

Joyce Baker later joined The Vernon's Girls who starred in many television shows, and is now – Mrs. Marty Wilde!

The rivalry between Terry and Marty was always friendly, but there was one time when Marty would have had just cause to come down from the stage at a concert in which he was starring in London, and thump him.

He knew Terry was in the audience and took a break from singing his hits to say: "Ladies and gentlemen, we have a great artist in the audience tonight – Terry Dene."

The audience went wild – and so did Marty. He explained: "Terry stood up to acknowledge the applause, and then instead of sitting down again, got up on to his seat and stood there saluting the crowd like a victorious boxer.

"He just stood, and stood, and stood! There was an incredible commotion for nearly 10 minutes."

Thrilled at his reception, Terry reluctantly got down from his seat and Marty tried to start singing again. But nobody listened, and feeling guilty, Terry decided he had done enough damage for one night, and got up and left.

Marty had a good laugh when he recounted the story, but the rivalry between various rock artists in those days was very real.

One of Terry's earliest fans was Harry Webb, the 17-year-old singer struggling with his group "The Drifters" for pop recognition. Webb knew Lincoln's *Two I's* was the only place to be heard and was only too glad to do a week's spot on the tiny stage; their cab fare home was the only fee.

"I was singing my heart out one night and getting nowhere, when Terry Dene walked in to see what was going on," he told me. "All the girls screamed like mad. They just didn't want to know us. It was uproar.

"Terry was persuaded to sing and he had the girls screaming their heads off.

"When he finished we started up again, but they ignored us. All they wanted was more from Terry."

Star-struck Harry – now Cliff Richard - later shook Terry's hand warmly, confessing: "It's a great pleasure, Mr. Dene. I've always wanted to meet you."

Little did the two singers know at that time that they would soon reverse roles in the popularity polls – or that they would both come to share a common faith.

During his first variety tour, Terry went round the country with *The Vipers*, top skiffle group of the time, and also *Two I's* discoveries. And again he nearly got thumped, this time by Wally Whyton of *The Vipers*, because of the timing of his entrance one night.

"Terry liked drama, and this night was no exception," Wally said. "He was due to finish the first half of the show, and we were scheduled to top the bill. About half an hour before Terry was due on, there was no sign of him.

"Naturally there was a panic backstage and I was told to get the group ready to go on instead.

"Seething with anger, I went round the pubs rounding up the group, and they rushed off to put on make-up.

"Minutes before he was due on, Terry casually strolled into the theatre, stopped and said with a smile, 'Do not fear, Dene is here.' I felt like smashing him!"

*

Terry was already beginning to exhibit the weaknesses in his character that were going to cause such havoc in later years. But little of this was publicised – in fact the Press began boosting him in earnest.

"For the teenage boy from the Buildings, life could not be better," read the fans.

"Record artist, music hall bill-topper, a film part, an American tour in the offing, 500 members in his month-old fan club. 'Now people look up to me and it feels good,' says Terry Dene. 'I'm going places and meeting people I never dreamed about a year ago.'

"People, for instance, like the Glasgow millionaire's 18-year-old grand-daughter who phones Terry every day. 'I met her last week,' he says. 'We've become very friendly, since. She's the most marvellous girl I've met'..."

One venue Terry and the group visited during this time wasn't so ritzy: Wormwood Scrubs Prison.

"It was quite a reunion for us," said manager Lincoln. "We found many of the lads inside were customers from the *Two I's*! Terry spent part of the concert saying 'hello' to them."

Terry began working at a pace nobody could have kept up for long but his showmanship was forged in this crucible of one-night stands. The tedium of the daily routine of travel was made worthwhile when he went on-stage and the fans went wild.

Exhaustion was never far from Terry. Clem Cattini recalls the occasion when Terry nearly fell from an express train because of it.

"We had been playing in Sheffield, and followed this with a week at Blackpool," he said. "A minibus took us to London first of all. We travelled from 10 p.m. to 10 a.m. the next morning.

"Then we caught a train from London to Blackpool. By then we were all fighting to keep awake. As the train roared north Terry said he wanted to go to the toilet. Not realising we were in a compartment with no corridor, he opened the door and nearly fell out. I just grabbed him in time. Otherwise there would have been no star of the show for the following week ...."

When Terry did break down in public he sent shock waves through the ranks of his fans. One time he had opened a shop, surrounded by screaming fans, and had been given an £18 radio for his efforts. He regarded this as a prized possession and took it back to his dressing room, looking forward to listening to it after the show.

But when he got to the stage door, yelling fans converged on him, knocking his radio to the floor and smashing it to bits.

For several minutes Terry blasted forth a torrent of Anglo-Saxon words. He lost a few fans that night.

Another time, outside Finsbury Park Empire, an incident occurred which could have been serious.

As Terry came out of the theatre, Mrs. Williams was there to greet him. A car was waiting nearby. As Terry made for the car, the crowd raced after him and his mother was hurled to the ground. Several of the stampeding youngsters trampled on her but it was only when Terry had reached the car that he realised what had happened. Again the air was blue and his mother received a stern warning from him not to risk life and limb again by standing at a stage door.

A year before he had been a record packer; now he was a recording star. And Terry was finding the attention and adulation a big cross to bear.

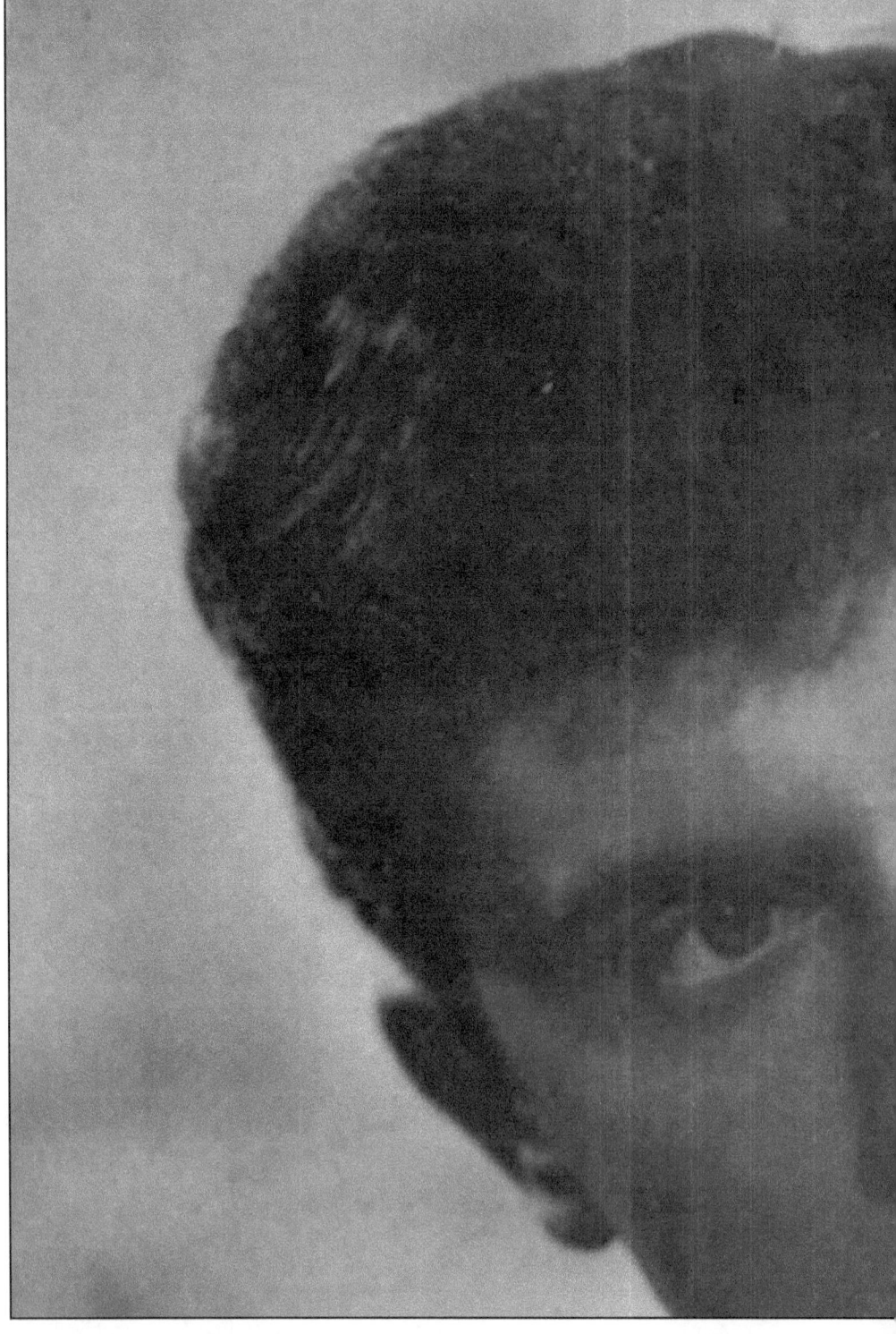

Chapter 8

Terry was giving one of the greatest performances of his life. He rocked and raved and rolled. But it didn't cut any ice with his one man audience. He just stared at him rather bleakly and snapped: "Get lost!"

The little old tramp huddled in a shop doorway just off Oxford Street that freezing late December morning had every right to wish Terry in a warmer place. For he had been woken up at three o'clock in the morning and offered a swig from an almost empty brandy bottle, and then given a private cabaret show starring the one and only, and very drunk, Terry Dene.

Cabaret show? It was a one-man spectacular, because despite the icy weather Terry was wearing only his underpants and carpet slippers!

It was his first Christmas away from mum and dad and he had decided to let his hair down.

Terry was staying at Lincoln's plush Wigmore Street flat and until then had not put a foot wrong. Lincoln was delighted with his new money-spinner and had sat back to watch the cash and congratulations roll in.

He had just got in bed for an early night when the bedside phone burred impatiently.

"Hello," he said, switching on a light. "Oh, it's you, Terry."

"Look, Paul. I'm in this club with Brian Gregg, you know, one of the Vipers." Terry paused. "Well – Paul, it's like this, we've got these two birds and I wondered if we could bring them round for a few drinks?"

Paul sighed, but he was feeling generous. "Certainly, Terry, go right ahead, but don't make too much noise."

The foursome, let in by Terry's key, giggled their way to the drinks cabinet. Terry was happy. A few drinks at the club had relaxed him and he felt at east with his "bird", a peroxide blonde who wouldn't have looked twice at him if he hadn't been the latest craze with six strings and two feet.

"Like a drink, baby?" Terry drawled, pausing by an unopened bottle of Martini. "Paul said we could help ourselves, so let's have a ball."

He filled the girl's glass to the brim and took a swig from the bottle himself. His head spun dizzily for a moment as he gasped for breath. "Boy, that's good!" He took another swig and then another.

"Lay off the drink, Terry," murmured a concerned Gregg.

"Mind your own business, I'm the star, not you. I'll drink what I like. You just plonk a guitar; I sing. They pay to hear ME!"

"Terry, keep your voice down, you'll wake Paul."

But Terry wasn't listening, he was emptying the rest of the bottle in one big swig. As it slid down he swayed from side to side.

"Ever seen drinking like that, baby?" he said, grinning stupidly at Miss Peroxide Blonde. "Well, sweety, you ain't seen nothing yet."

With that the inebriated idol opened another gleaming Martini bottle and proceeded to guzzle down the contents, with just a brief pause to wipe his dripping lips.

As the drink disappeared, so did most of Terry's clothes. "I feel like stripping," he yelled drunkenly as the two girls gasped. "And neither you, nor anybody else is going to stop me!" Socks, shirt, vest, trousers ballooned across the room at the dumbstruck guests, and Terry grabbed a bottle of brandy and rushed out into the icy night.

After his brush with the tramp, the near-naked pop idol staggered off in search of other revellers, the brandy bottle at his lips. Suddenly he caught sight of a first-floor window with lights blazing. Through an alcoholic haze he saw people moving about. At first the drink made him merry. Now he was turning bitter and suddenly he hated them all. "Why am I always on the outside?" he yelled, holding his spinning head in his hands. The words reverberated round the street. "Why ... always outside ..."

Hate burned inside him. He picked up three no-waiting signs one after the other and slung them through a tobacconist's window. Glass splintered noisily, splaying across the road and in among the display of pipes and tobacco.

Terry staggered across the pavement almost completely immobilised by bottles of Martini and swigs of brandy. For several minutes he battled to stay upright, then made his way to a builder's hut and pleaded with the frightened night watchman to call the cops. Soon a police car screeched to the side of the pavement and out jumped two officers.

"Thank goodness you're here," Terry gasped. "I'm freezing."

The sergeant looked at him in disgust. "Idiot," he hissed and shoved Terry into the back seat with a tunic wrapped round his shoulders.

At West End Central police station, a doctor was called in to examine him. "He's lucky to be alive," Terry heard him say. "He's drunk enough to sink a battleship."

Brian frantically shook the sleeping figure of Paul Lincoln; Terry had been away for a quarter of an hour.

"What's up?" slurred the big man, shielding his eyes from the artificial light. "What's ... it's not morning yet, is it?"

"Paul, it's serious. Terry's drunk two bottles of Martini and run out in the near altogether. He hasn't come back."

Screaming press headlines suddenly rolled across Lincoln's mind. TERRY DENE RUNS NAKED AND DRUNK ... He could see it all too plainly. "What am I going to do?" he asked desperately.

"Find him before it's too late, Paul, before he does something daft."

Still dressed only in his pyjamas, Lincoln fumbled in his coat for his wallet, drew out a couple of crisp pound notes and handed them to the girls. "Get a taxi home, girls. Sorry the evening's been spoiled, but get off home quickly, and keep this to yourself."

The girls were only too glad to make their escape and rushed from the flat, followed shortly by Lincoln who was so over-wrought he forgot to get dressed and dashed out into the night in his pyjamas to try to reclaim his rising star before he cashed in an explosion of bad publicity.

A quick search of nearby streets revealed nothing so he returned shivering to the flat. He was fuming and coldly working out a plan of torture for the wayward boy, when there was a knock on his front door.

"Are you Mr. Lincoln?" A policeman was standing squarely on the doorstep. "The Mr. Lincoln who looks after Terry Dene?"

He paused as the *Two I's* man nodded, and waited for the worst.

"I wonder if you would mind accompanying me to the station, sir. You see, Mr. Dene requires your help." He added with an embarrassed cough, "I would be obliged if you would put some clothes on, Mr. Lincoln."

"Oh, I'm sorry," Lincoln threw off his night clothes and was soon properly attired and tucked into the warm police car. The officer was considerate and he felt better. The end of the world had not yet come, after all.

Terry sat shivering in his shadowy cell. He was convinced the end HAD come. The effect of the alcohol was wearing off and the stark reality of what he had done hit him hard. As the footsteps of his burly manager echoed down the corridor leading to his temporary home, Terry drew the blanket tightly round him and waited ...

"Look, Paul, I'm very sorry, it was the drink ..."

Paul had worked out a plan of verbal attack with which he was going to crush Terry, but when he saw his pea-green face and appealing, though blood-shot, eyes, he melted.

"Look, Terry, I don't know what happened to you, but I just hope this doesn't spoil your chances. I'll get on to a publicist friend and see if he can smooth this over."

Lincoln's friend told him nothing could be done to prevent the case going in the papers, but suggested it would look good if they paid for the damage.

The Press bench was crowded that morning. Word had flashed around Fleet Street news desks that the new sensation was – a new sensation.

Terry pleaded "guilty" to being, as Mr. Clyde Wilson, the Marlborough Street magistrate, described it "mad drunk" in a Mayfair street. He was fined £2. He also pleaded guilty to causing malicious damage – and for that he was conditionally discharged.

The *Daily Mirror*, along with most of the national dailies, carried the tale and featured pictures of the pasty-faced singer. "I'M ON THE WATER WAGON NOW, SAYS TERRY DENE" the *Mirror* headlines declared. "We had been celebrating the birthday of one of the boys in the band," he was reported as saying as he sipped milk in a Soho café. "It was a pretty wild night, and I can only remember bits of what happened."

"Before I threw the signs through the window I felt I was going to do something stupid. I did not feel at all cold – not with what I had inside me," he added.

The incident, however, had its funny side. Paul Lincoln told me: "I had to guarantee to the tobacconist's that they would get full compensation for the damage caused to the window and their pipe stock. This was the only way we could prevent Terry getting into more serious trouble.

"The bill was huge, and included a claim for a large quantity of supposedly damaged pipes, some costing about £22 each.

"I contacted them immediately and said: 'If you're going to charge me for all these pipes, I want them.'

"They were a bit taken aback, but later agreed to deliver all the 'damaged' pipes to me.

"For weeks afterwards I was handing out £22 pipes to all my friends and contacts. We had a ball smoking ourselves silly!"

Chapter 9

It was as Terry Dene stood at the side of the stage in a Peterborough theatre, waiting for his spot, that he first saw Edna Savage singing. She had a school-girl figure and the lights shone on her face, an upturned golden profile.

He thought she was the most beautiful thing he had ever seen, and immediately fell head over heels in love with her.

But the brilliance of the stage electrician in making her into an unobtainable angel that night resulted in heartbreak for petite Edna.

Once a telephonist in Warrington, she was now a rising star with a horde of male admirers, appeared regularly in the "Six-Five Special" and was seemingly set for a long and successful singing career.

After she met Terry Dene it all gradually crumbled. And it's been heartbreak all the way, with her third marriage now apparently on the rocks. She told me in September 1973 that husband Doug Wilkes, 10 years younger than Edna, was no longer living with her and their twin daughters. She revealed that at one stage she mixed a "suicide cocktail" of sleeping tablets – but changed her mind when she thought about her 19-month-old twins.

Her second marriage, to car dealer Reginald Rose in 1964, lasted five years. During that marriage her baby son died after five days. She was advised not to have children again but after marrying Doug she spent 12 weeks in hospital to have the twins. One got pneumonia. The other struggled for life with meningitis. Life's been tough since she met Terry Dene.

But back in the fifties she was a carefree golden girl. Terry was completely infatuated, and began to spend all his spare time with Edna. On the second day at Peterborough, a Tuesday, she mentioned she was going to the pictures. Terry asked if he could go along.

They saw *The Pride and the Passion*, but Terry wasn't paying much attention to the screen. He kept sneaking looks at the profile that had captivated him. Then she turned her head slowly and looked straight at him. They kissed.

For the rest of the week's run, Terry could hardly tear himself away from Edna's dressing-room to go in front of the paying customers, and they spent every minute off stage together.

The next week they were delighted to find they were both on the same bill at Gloucester. Terry was picking up £400 and Edna £175 – not bad for a couple of teenagers.

"But when you mix young love with that kind of money something's got to give," said Terry later.

It gave all right.

After falling for Edna, Terry got to wondering how it would all end. He began to think of the complications ... the damage marriage could do for his career.

And while he was sitting about gnawing his nails, Edna was doing some thinking too.

"How can we ever make a go of marriage if we're appearing at opposite ends of the country?" she asked Terry. "When will we ever get to see each other?"

Edna said she wasn't sure if she wanted him, but Terry was absolutely convinced he wanted her. He hoped they would be booked together, but Edna wasn't convinced.

After the first night in Gloucester, he went back to his hotel in a black mood and had a meal on his own. He downed just a few drinks, but, as always, drink proved dynamite.

He swore later he didn't have enough "to make a cat drunk", but the alcohol triggered off the savage streak which he couldn't control.

Terry walked around the streets and finally ended up outside Edna's hotel room. He kicked the door open, and rocked into the room singing "You'll Never Know Just How Much I Love You". His face was ashen.

But his dramatic entrance didn't go down as well as he had hoped. Sitting in bed, Edna looked up from the magazine she was reading and said disapprovingly: "And what do you want at this time of night?"

"I had to see you," he said, again bursting into song. "You'll Never Know How Much I Love You ..."

"Oh, grow up, Terry," she said, turning her attention back to the magazine.

Her rejection provoked a volcano in Terry. He walked up to the wall and smashed his fist into it. He picked up a cane wastepaper basket and tore it apart. He kicked at the bedclothes and ripped them from the bed. Then he punched the mirror, causing flesh to shred from his hand.

A startled Edna quickly dropped her magazine. This wasn't the Terry she knew. As he looked for something else to wreck, she rushed across the room in panic, but he swung round and his elbow jabbed into her left eye.

Terry dived onto the bed and held on to the mattress. He held it tight, trying to stop himself from doing more damage.

Edna thought he was going to have a fit.

"Get the manager," he told her. "I'm not feeling very well."

His hand was pouring with blood, and he was trembling all over.

A panic-stricken Edna flew out of the door.

"For God's sake, someone get a doctor," she yelled.

Terry lay on the bed writhing and crying like a baby. But when the manager came in, Terry recovered and ran from the room. He ran and ran until he got to a nearby hospital.

A cool but efficient nurse bandaged his bloody hand and told him to wait while she fetched a doctor.

Terry sat in a room off the casualty department, staring up at the bare, antiseptic walls. But after a few minutes, he got up and struggled into his jacket. No one made any attempt to stop him as he walked down a long, green-painted corridor and out into the cold night.

A woman who saw Terry said later: "He was staggering along. I didn't know whether he was ill or drunk."

The light of a telephone kiosk beckoned him into the empty street. He went into the booth to phone Edna at the hotel, but hadn't got enough pennies. So he smashed the receiver and kicked in a glass panel.

Further down the road, he picked up two motor-cycles and threw them around for a bit. He was working off some of the hate inside him for everyone who was asleep in a world where, it seemed, only Terry Dene suffered.

As he marched moodily into the centre of Gloucester, past the giant posters of himself, he left a trail of wreckage behind. He managed to kick in two plate-glass windows before a police car roared into the kerb beside him.

Heaven alone knows where Gloucestershire Constabulary found their patience.

"I'm not really drunk ... It's Edna, I love her ... she rejected me ... it's not my fault."

"O.K. son. Calm down."

After Terry was charged, Lincoln was contacted and came rushing from London. "I'll kill that boy," he told Hymie after receiving the call. "He'll be the death of us both."

"I can't understand why he should do these things. He's usually such a nice boy," said Zahl sadly. Lincoln made the journey in record time, strode into the police station and was immediately taken to the cells to see Terry. He found his wayward star playing on the floor with a stray dog, brought in shortly before Terry.

"We thought it would help him to have a bit of company," explained an officer.

Lincoln's murderous thoughts dissolved when he saw Terry with his arm around the scraggy dog. "Couple of strays together," he muttered.

The incident cost Terry £155 in fines, plus £112 for the damage. It also cost him contracts worth about £6,000 and landed him in the hands of the head-shrinkers.

The Press splashed the happening. The *Daily Mail* headlined it: "MIDNIGHT HOTEL SCENE, A DAY IN THE CELLS, THEN TEENAGE IDOL SAYS 'I'M ILL'." *The Times* had "YOUNG SINGER 'WENT BERSERK', PITCHFORKED INTO LIFE OF PUBLICITY."

Terry pleaded guilty in court to three wilful damage charges, but not guilty to being drunk and disorderly, and that charge was withdrawn.

"I had an argument and a few drinks," ran Terry's statement to the police. "I had one too many and wanted to be destructive. I went and smashed a few windows. I don't know why I did it, but I suppose the influence of the drinks made me destructive."

His lawyer offered sincere apologies, and said that Terry had comparatively little to drink and it looked as if his background was contributory to what happened.

Until early the year before, he said, 'Terry had led a quiet life. He discovered he could sing in a manner which was popular, and was more or less pitchforked into a life of publicity. This meant tension, excitement and great strain to anyone not accustomed to appearing in public.

On the night of the incident he was suffering from great emotional stress. He drank a whisky and half a bottle of white wine with his supper and after that the trouble started. He became hysterical and began to beat the walls of the room, and still bore the bruises and cuts on his hands. He was taken to hospital, then he went berserk.

A leading psychiatrist said that an institute of psychiatry in London was willing to examine Dene as a matter of urgency.

The Chairman of the Bench told Terry: "We suggest you cultivate a sense of proportion and try to face your responsibilities ... In view of your youth we shall not send you to prison. We hope you will take advantage of the medical suggestions which have been made."

After the case, most of the national newspapers had a field day. The *Daily Express* carried a king-size feature which included, "MY BOY TERRY, BY HIS MOTHER", "I WILL STAND BY TERRY, SAYS EDNA", "TERRY DENE, BY TERRY DENE", "TERRY DENE, BY THE POLICE", "TERRY DENE BY A LAWYER", "TERRY DENE, BY THE GIRL", "TERRY DENE, BY THE AGENTS".

Edna was reported by the *Express* to have said: "It is very hard for any variety artist. You are not able to relax. You cannot afford to have an off-day; otherwise people say nasty things about you. You have to be on your guard all the time trying to be nice and bright.

"The moment I met Terry, about two weeks ago, I thought 'This kid has got something.'

"But he is a sick man and needs attention. He had been going about all over the place, working hard and getting very little sleep. One could see the strain he was under – and it is a strain at the top. He is not quite mature enough yet, and can't take it mentally and emotionally. But he will. His trouble is he is far too sincere and conscientious. All this popularity, with all the girls after him, has affected him a lot. It has not gone to his head – in fact, it is the other way about. He is really a very unassuming type, but all this glamour was such a change for him."

Because of the court case, Terry was taken off the bill and replaced by Tommy Steele's brother, Colin Hicks.

The *Daily Mail* talked to Terry after the case, back at his hotel. "I've not seen my agent yet, but tell my fans that this rest is what I need to get fit."

Sitting beside him as he ate a late lunch was Edna. She removed her dark glasses to show the reporter a one-inch bruise under her left eye.

"You need this steak more than I do," laughed Terry, as they talked. He went on to tap his forehead with the handle of his knife, saying: "It's up here I feel it. If the people behind me wouldn't try and push me so hard, I'd be all right. They've got to realise I'm a human being, not a machine."

Meanwhile Zahl was reported to have said at his Piccadilly office: "I have seen this coming for some time. Terry's a strange boy."

Terry was due to appear at Norwich the following week. His place was taken by Marty Wilde. "Now there's a boy who's going to be really big," said Hymie's brother, Sonnie.

But although Terry's love affair with Edna had got off to a dreadful start, he went back to his parents' seventh-floor flat in Camberwell to find messages scrawled in lipstick across his car. "I love you, Terry," they said. And "Get well soon."

Meanwhile Edna bravely continued with her spot in the show at Gloucester. Her songs included "Cock-eyed Optimist", and "Ma, He's Making Eyes At Me", which naturally went down well with the customers.

Chapter 10

Bill Haley's film, *Rock Around the Clock*, was a smash in every sense of the word.

All over Britain, Teddy Boys wearing drainpipe trousers, three-quarter-length jackets, brothel-creepers, and string-ties, slashed cinema seas and wrecked theatres as the man with the kiss curl rocked across the screen. Many towns banned the film completely: its violence crystallised the teenage rock rebellion here.

Terry Dene's first film, *The Golden Disc,* which followed close on its heels, had a different reception.

Cinemas were packed with screaming love-struck girls who had queued for hours for the privilege of yelling at their idol's image on the screen.

But they weren't there to make trouble. Many jived in the aisles, and after each number, the fans stood and applauded.

I spoke to a former Teddy Boy, now a successful businessman, who was forced to see the film at an East End cinema four times in one week.

"My girl friend dragged me along to our local picture house in the Mile End Road nearly every night during the week-long run," he said. "The only reason we went was that she was madly in love with Terry Dene. I knew it and she knew it, but neither of us spoke about it.

"Mind you, I wasn't complaining – I had a good time as well. Every time Terry did something sexy on the screen, she grabbed me and gave me a whopping big kiss!

"I knew she was pretending I was Terry, but who was I to complain? I had a ball!"

The film, made at Walton Studios, Surrey, included in its cast Lee Patterson, Mary Steele, Linda Fray and Ronald Adam. Besides Terry, a host of musical artistes appeared – Dennis Lotis, Nancy Whiskey, Les Hobeaux, Murray Campbell, Sheila Buxton, the Phil *Seamon Jazz Group*, Sonny Stewart and his Skiffle Kings and the *Terry Kennedy Group*; fortunately, Mickie Most was not hired as an extra this time!

The Golden Disc had the usual flimsy story of three struggling performers finding fame in the record business and Dene hitting the jackpot with a gold disc.

A review in the *News of the World* said: "I am sure that crowds of coffee-bar cats will line up for the fiesta, but I confess I found my own thoughts straying to the real-life Terry Dene."

The end of the film meant a mass pocketing of damp handkerchiefs by weeping girls, a pledge of undying love for their Golden Boy, and a rush for the exits before too much of the National Anthem trapped them.

During filming, Terry decided it would be good for his image to own a big car, so he took time off to visit Rootes' plush showrooms in Piccadilly and selected a two-tone blue Humber Super Snipe with white-walled tyres.

Because he only had a learner's licence, the driving was done by drummer Clem Cattini, but Terry soon got fed up with being chauffeured everywhere in his new toy. So he rebelled, clambered into the driving seat, started the engine, and, despite protests from the rest of the group, zig-zagged his way up the street, a broad grin on his face.

Fortunately, the police weren't' around and he was not involved in an accident, so this time he got away without a court appearance or Press coverage: a rare happening indeed for Terry Dene.

But back to the film. Butcher's, who made the movie, decided to dish out Terry Dene badges to fans to promote it. "Terry Dene's popularity among teenagers all over the country is quite extraordinary when one considers that he had been in show business for such a short time," said the brochure sent to cinema managers.

"A short while ago Dene-age badges were introduced to his London fans. The idea met with phenomenal success, and Terry was inundated with requests for fresh supplies to be sent to his fan clubs all over the country. Now, if you visit a theatre where Terry is topping the bill, you will find that almost everyone under 21 is a Dene-ager.

"We feel certain that if you order a quantity of these badges a great deal of local publicity would be obtained. They could be issued at a small charge, or even free of charge, to all teenagers who visit your theatre."

Decca Records issued an EP record of the film which features four of Terry's songs, "C'mon and be Loved", "Golden Age", "Charm", and "Candy Floss", and two 78s with other songs.

The film also helped Terry to acquire a new friend, Nemone Lethbridge, the glamorous barrister daughter of Major-General John Lethbridge, formerly Chief of Intelligence, Rhine Army, who later defended Ronnie Kray and Frank Mitchell, the so-called "Mad Axe-Man".

In fact Oxford graduate Miss Lethbridge, called to the Bar in June 1956, accompanied Terry to the première of his film at the Rialto Cinema. She was clinging to his arm as they entered the foyer in the flare of flash-bulbs. Terry, wearing a light blue drape suit and grey suede shoes, laughed and told reporters, "She is just a very good friend of mine."

And Nemone, in white lace, added "Terry and his mother and father invited me, and I'm very pleased to be here." A friend of Terry's said, "She wrote Terry several letters during his recent troubles."

Nemone was no stranger to the headline writers. In 1954, while still at Oxford, she launched and edited *Couth* – as opposed to uncouth. She described it as a magazine to express the university's "exquisite approach to life". Its articles included "smart" words then current such as "gusting" as opposed to disgusting, and "pulsive" rather than impulsive.

But according to the *Daily Mail*, Miss Lethbridge didn't have a word to describe the frenzied chantings of 100 teenagers, all members of the Terry Dene fan club, who waited outside the cinema for an hour.

When the couple stepped from their car, Terry merely waved to the girls.

The *Mail* contacted Nemone's mother at her home in Frome, Somerset, for comment; she was reported to have responded: "Terry Dene? I don't think I've ever heard of him. My daughter is certainly not his barrister. No, I'm sorry, I just don't know anything about this."

The friendship between these two opposites attracted a lot of publicity. Louis Kirby wrote in the *Daily Mail*, "Nemone Lethbridge, at 25 the belle of the Bar, counsel for the prosecution and friend of teenage idol Terry Dene, took off her wig and gown and told me yesterday 'I am terribly fond of rock 'n' roll.' The news went round the wigged heads in Court No. 3 that Terry Dene had escorted Nemone to the premiere of his film *The Golden Disc*.

"Hazel-eyed Nemone sighed and said, 'I do hope people will understand that there is no romance between us. I like him, we have eaten out together and I have bought every record he has made. He has wonderful talent and a fine voice, but could say my interest is academic.

"'I am fascinated by the rock 'n' roll phenomenon which comes into my forthcoming book on juvenile delinquency. I decided to go out to meet the new demi-gods. Now I am rather bound up in their world.

"'Tommy Steele I found very attractive, his brother Colin Hicks a chirpy sparrow and entirely unsquashable, Marty Wilde just incomprehensible ... but Terry, he's different. We have some very intelligent discussions, and I have known him come out with some quite Hamlet-like remarks!'"

Nemone told Louis Kirby she met Terry six months before and became interested in him in a "clinical sort of way".

"When he was prosecuted recently for being drunk and doing damage, he needed a shoulder to cry on, and came to me. For a while I teased him but I also tried to comfort Terry, because I realised he was a mixed-up juvenile, flung into a world right out of his depth. I wrote him several letters, too, but merely from friendship.

"His father, whom I also like very much, came to my chambers to discuss Terry with me, and he it was who asked me to back him up by going to that wretched première." Nemone added, "Terry is sweet and intelligent and, strange though it may seem, we have some quite deep conversations."

It was all good stuff for the fans to read on their way to work; but for Terry there was only one girl – Edna Savage.

Chapter 11

'm sick, sick, sick – sick of being hounded, sick of the lime-light, sick of the pressure – in fact, just plain mentally sick! What's wrong with me? You tell me – I don't know. I wish I did.

"I've tried to work it out and I can't. So I'm going to the experts to find out – let them do the worrying for me. It's their job and they're good at it, so I'm told. They might not be much good at rock 'n' roll, but I'm no doctor either."

It was the Sunday after Terry's Gloucester blow-up, and the now defunct *Empire News* was carrying his "frank confessions". He was waiting to go into hospital and his affair with Edna was apparently at an end.

"I know what people are saying about me – that success has gone to my head; that I can't take it; that I'm getting more money than is good for me," he told the readers. "All right! Let them say it. But I sometimes wonder what they would have done if they had found themselves in my shoes these last 12 months? Curled up and died most likely.

"I made one big mistake just when everything was going fine. Now I've done it again. After the lesson I had that first time, and the fright it gave me, you'd think I would be only too keen to keep my record straight. That's why I think there's something wrong with me – and I want to find out what it is.

"Get it straight, I'm ill! And all the £25,000 or more they reckon I earn a year – you can have it. I'm going into a nursing home – the only thing I worry about now is getting Terry Dene straight with Terry Dene.

"In the last year I've crammed in more than a lot of people do in a lifetime. I've been on the go all the time and I discovered that the bright lights, the gay parties, meeting famous men and pretty girls, the money, my name in lights ... they don't mean a thing! All I want right now is some roots somewhere. I want a home to go back to – a home I know belongs to me and will always be there when I want it.

TERRY DENE: BRITAIN'S FIRST ROCK AND ROLL REBEL

"All I want is peace, peace, peace – peace of mind, time to think."

All this was in 1958; but it would be many years before Terry found the peace he so desired.

He added, "People yap an awful lot about teenagers – but how many really try to understand what we are thinking and feeling? What clicks with their own kids – never mind anybody else's. I'm like a lot of other teenagers and I've got the same problems. Only I'm stuck up there for everyone to look at, and, believe me, that's not all honey."

Terry went on to outline what he felt was the source of his mental problems. "I've said I've got problems. Not about how to make money, or films, or best-selling records, but simply how to live. Maybe if you're tough and haven't any nerves you can take this business. But I've got nerves. I always have had, and so has my Mum. Which is why I don't blame show business for all my troubles.

"Whatever's wrong with me may have started ages ago, when our home was being bombed. When the ceiling fell in one night. Or the day I found myself locked in an air-raid shelter and nobody knew I was there. I nearly went mad before they let me out."

While Terry was getting himself "sorted out" by a psychiatrist, Paul Lincoln and Hymie Zahl were tearing their hair out, for Terry's antics were costing them money – big money.

The first major blow came when the promoter of a South African tour suddenly cancelled it. Terry had been booked for the tour at £1,000 a week, but he was suddenly informed that he would not be allowed to enter the Union. The promoter of the tour, Mr. Ken Park, told the Press that he had received an intimation to this effect from the Department of the Interior. The ban was believed to be due to public feeling aroused by recent rock 'n' roll disturbances, though little trouble had been experienced during the visit of Tommy Steele, whose presence had also excited opposition in some centres.

Lincoln told me, "We had the contract in black and white. It was to be £1,000 a week and first-class air fares for all of us. The news was enough to make Lew and Leslie Grade vomit."

Then a lucrative film part was cancelled, and that hurt even more.

"A group of us including Terry was invited to a posh party in Kensington after one of his shows at the Finsbury Park Empire," he said. "At the party I met a young chap who had seen Terry on *Six-Five Special* and thought he was great. He said his father, a famous film producer, wanted to give him a part in a film and would call me about it."

The producer did ring Paul and invited him and Terry over to his office. Paul went in on his own first of all and was told "I can't follow these trends today, but my son and his friends love this *Six-Five Special* programme and they say that Terry Dene is the greatest thing in this world."

After a chat with Terry he told Lincoln, "It's a deal!"

That was before the Gloucester fracas. Then the letter arrived. "Under the circumstances we regret ..."

Lincoln was coming to the conclusion that his *Two I's* coffee-bar was a better financial prospect than his rock 'n' roll singer. He was heavily criticised, but hit back in an interview with the *Daily Express*.

"Why does everyone try to make me out as a villain?" he said, puffing his cigar. "I know Terry's parents think I'm a villain. And I know they are not the only ones. But I have certainly done nothing wrong. Look, Terry wanted to get to the top and me and Hymie got him there. It's ridiculous to say he was pushed. You've got to work hard in this business.

"He's been on about £500 a week these last few weeks before his crack-up. I took 30% and Hymie 10%. But I had to pay for a lot out of my share, fan club, someone to tour with him, other expenses. Not so long ago I was £1,000 out of pocket on him, and I still haven't made it up. What's more, I have been locked out of my flat because I had Terry sleeping there at week-ends – I'm taking legal action on that.

"To me he is a piece of property into which I have sunk a lot of money. Now I naturally want the maximum return. Hymie and I have him under contract for five years and I have no intention of dropping him."

Clem told me: "Paul was one of the straightest men I've ever worked for, and he tried to do everything for the best for Terry."

Meanwhile, as the rows continued, Terry got on with long sessions with a psychiatrist to track down what was wrong. In a newspaper interview after his first visit he said, "The psychiatrist tells me it was really the air raids in the war which started my trouble. They meant a lot of work for my mother, who loved me but didn't have all the time she wanted to look after me the way she wanted to. So I got to feel as if I was being pushed away – not wanted. It wasn't true – but that's the way I felt.

"I found all that out the first two or three days I went to the psychiatrist ... and I felt better right away. He's told me if I want to talk to him about anything at any time – it doesn't matter where I am or when it is – all I've got to do is phone and get it off my chest. To have someone around like that takes the weight off your shoulders," he added. " ... Makes you feel free again."

But things did not turn out the way he hoped. At first it was decided he would not have to go to hospital, and for a time he was happy spending an hour each day talking to the "head doctor". As he was not working, he was left with a lot of time on his hands. A lot of time to think ... and to hang around. It gave him a chance to see some of his old pals, and to do quite a bit of thinking ... about show business and the cost of fame. And that did him no good at all, so he was admitted to hospital.

"Perhaps one of the troubles with me is that I might have got too much too quickly," he said at the time, "and that trying to be the kind of person the kids think Terry Dene should be has turned me into a crazy mixed-up kid myself.

"I only hope I can sort myself out in a hurry. I've had two chances, which is one more than most people get. There might not be a third".

Chapter 12

Terry did sort himself out, for a time, at least, and Dick Rowe decided he was going to take a hand in ending the nightmare. He planned to steer the mixed-up record star back to the top.

He had already produced a string of hits for Terry, including "A White Sport Coat", "Teenage Dream", "Start Movin'", "Stairway of Love", "Seven Steps to Love", "Who Baby Who", but he knew the bad publicity had sapped Terry's confidence.

Rowe arranged for the 19-year-old rock star to make his comeback at London's Empress Hall in front of 7,000 fans. The date was the "Record Star Show", presented by the *Daily Express* in association with the Stars Organisation for Spastics.

For weeks, the record wizard had Terry in his office at Decca and went through a routine with him. He arranged with orchestra leader Cyril Stapleton for Terry to sing a medley of his hits – and not stop for a moment, in case he dried up.

"I know you're nervous, Terry," said Rowe, leaning back in his chair, "but you've got the talent to knock them out. Do just that.

"Now let's go over those songs again ..."

Lincoln and Zahl left Dick Rowe to get on with Terry's grooming, confident he would instil in the boy the ability to make a successful comeback.

On the night of the show, Terry was more nervous than ever before. He peeped through the curtains as the audience filed in, and gasped.

"I can't sing in front of all those people," he told Rowe,

"They'll laugh at me. They've all read about the silly things I've been doing lately."

"Terry, just go on and be yourself. Nobody's going to laugh."

It was a new Terry Dene who walked on stage that night. His hair was cropped short and he was wearing a smart grey suit. It was a different act, too. There was no rock 'n' roll quartet to support. No wild stomping around the stage.

Nobody screamed, but the welcoming applause was deafening as he walked to the microphone. He stood for a moment and then looked at Cyril Stapleton, who lifted his baton and signalled the start of the 15-minute spot.

"I didn't want him to pause for a moment," Dick Rowe told me. "I knew it would be disastrous if he did – his nerves would have taken over. He sang number after number without a mistake. It was a faultless performance.

"The audience went wild as he finished his last song and dashed off stage and I went wild with excitement. There were tears in my eyes, because he had done it. It was a very proud moment for me, and for Terry."

As the singer stumbled off stage, in a daze, he collapsed into Rowe's arms. Both were shaking with emotion.

Terry soon recovered and breathlessly told an *Express* reporter: "It was just the excitement of getting such a warm welcome back. I'm sure I'll be all right."

Before he went on, he had told a journalist: "I'm a different character now. I'm off the psychiatrist's couch for good, I hope, and ready to go on with my career.

"I have five engagements lined up for this week already, so it looks as if I will be busy again.

"But I don't want to go back to where I was. I want it to be different this time."

The show, which also featured stars like Michael Holliday, Dickie Valentine, Alma Cogan, Marion Ryan, Vera Lynn, Kenneth Earl, Malcolm Vaughan, Ronnie Hilton, *The Stargazers* and comic Stan Stennett, raised £3,500 for the spastics.

It also raised the moral of Terry Dene sky-high.

That wasn't the only present Terry had, for Zahl decided he was fit enough to start again. A big tour of the country was laid on, and, to Terry's delight, he found Edna was on the same bill and, even better, was still talking to him.

"Look, Terry," she said. "I want to make it clear that we can remain friends, but it mustn't be serious. Anyway, I've got a new boyfriend. He's an actor, Andrew Ray."

Terry agreed to keep it platonic, but deep down resented his rival. And his anger boiled up when he walked into Edna's dressing-room one day when she was out to find an oil painting of her new boyfriend in a place of prominence. In a fit of anger, he whipped a penknife from his pocket and lunged at the canvas. He slashed and slashed at the picture in a frenetic rage until all that was left were some limp shreds of material.

When Edna came back she was horrified to see what had been done. Just then Terry strolled in.

"Sorry about that," he said casually. "Wasn't much of a picture though, was it?"

Edna was dumbfounded. She hadn't been in love with Andrew, son of comedian Ted Ray, but had accompanied him on several enjoyable dinner dates and described him to me as a "sweet, gentle, yet sophisticated boy".

"I didn't realise that Andrew was going through a particularly bad period in his life, smashing cars up, feeling lost in his acting career, and aware of a successful father and brother," she said.

"We saw a little of each other. There were dinner dates, red roses each day, and phone calls from him when he was in America. But when he realised I was booked to appear on a long run with Terry, he was furious. He left my home upset by the news.

"I was to leave for the north of England at 7 a.m. next day. At 4.30 a.m. my phone range and a nurse told me: 'A Mr. Andrew Ray has given me your telephone number. He's had an accident and has suffered face lacerations.' My heart sank, God, not another Terry, I thought.

"When I arrived at the hospital, Andrew was lying on a trolley. When he saw me he said in a dramatic voice: 'You shouldn't have come'. I thought, here we go again ..."

A face-to-face confrontation between the rivals nearly took place in a London cinema. Terry invited Edna to the pictures and she held his arm as they approached Leicester Square. Strollers in the street whispered, "There's Terry Dene and Edna Savage," but the couple took no notice. They were used to attracting attention.

Little did Edna know what was in store for her as she stepped into the cinema.

"We were guided to a couple of seats by an usherette," she told me. "But, because of the darkness, I didn't know where we were sitting, and by an incredible coincidence, I had been seated next to actor Andrew Ray, the son of comedian, Ted Ray.

"He didn't realise I was with Terry, and was flattered that I had come to sit by him. He tenderly took hold of my hand while Terry, engrossed in the film, grabbed my right hand!

"I sat in the middle, petrified, wondering what would happen when each discovered the other was there.

"The lights went up and Andrew looked at my pale face and then spotted Terry also holding my hand. At that very moment Terry saw him, and I turned to Andrew and hissed desperately, 'Get out quickly, and grab a taxi'.

"He got the message, scrambled for the exit and was off before Terry could do anything. It was a terrible experience, though looking back it sounds funny.

"I left with Terry, not Andrew, because Terry was the wild one and Andrew knew it. He backed out rather gracefully, I thought."

Edna did not see a lot of Andrew after that. "When I did meet up with him again he had matured into a lovely person." She feels today a lot of the troubles of artists like Andrew and Terry were because they had too much too early.

"It's a great pity that show-biz is so hung up on youth, but then perhaps irrational behaviour is part of this sad game."

But back to Terry Dene: Edna vividly remembered another of Terry's fits of jealousy. It happened when she started going out with a wealthy young aristocrat.

"He was really upper class and used to drive me around in his Bentley. Terry hated him," she told me.

"One day I told him to come to the stage door. I was used to the crowds of screaming teenagers hanging around stage doors for a glimpse of Terry, but this chap had never seen anything like it.

"Anyway, he fought his way through the crowd and told the commissionaire he had come to see me. He was expected at the door and so it was opened to let him in.

"But immediately my date walked in, a hosepipe was turned on him and he was knocked flying by the force of the water.

"A man had been stationed there to stop fans getting in and assumed this was another admirer trying to gatecrash. The poor chap was completely soaked!

"To make it worse, Terry was passing at the time and saw the whole thing. He fell apart laughing.

"When I later told this chap I had decided to pack him up for Terry, he said over the phone, 'I can forgive anything – but a rock 'n' roll singer!"

"It was the final humiliation for him!"

Terry and Edna's courtship, if you could call it that, was chequered to say the least. Countless times he proposed marriage and she refused.

Finally Edna agreed to an engagement, but then threatened to call if off and marry someone else.

Then Terry went on the bottle again. And this time he was nearly charged with murder.

Drinking heavily, he was crying on the shoulder of an old friend. "Edna won't have me," he wailed. "I'd do anything to get her back, but she says she never wants to see me again."

Because of his behaviour she had banned him for her flat.

Down went a double Scotch ... and another ... and another. By the time they got round to the second bottle, Terry's mood changed, and the self-pity went.

"I'm going round to see her ... I'll show her," he bellowed. "Who does she think she is treating me like this?"

Terry's friend tried to stop him, but he might as well have tried to put the brakes on a charging elephant. Terry was again out of control and heading for serious trouble.

When Edna arrived at her flat in Great Cumberland Place after a meal with singer Ronnie Carroll, she found a note pinned to the door which read: "I'M GOING TO KILL YOU, HA, HA, HA."

As she walked in the phone rang. It was a slurred Terry, warning her of his impending visit. Terrified, she immediately rang Ronnie and asked him to come round to protect her.

"I don't believe it," was Carroll's initial reaction.

"He might just try, Ronnie," said a desperate Edna, shaking with fear.

"O.K. I'll come."

Meanwhile Terry was lurching around nearby streets. Near Marble Arch a group of people, also very drunk, shouted across.

"You're Terry Dene, aren't you? Where are you going, Terry boy?"

As he kicked a newspaper stand into the gutter, he yelled back: "To kill Edna Savage, that's where."

The flat was dark when he arrived. There was no reply when he rang the bell, but he was certain she was inside.

"Open up, or I'll break down the door," he shouted through the letter-box, plus a few bits of choice language. Terry was a man of his word. He waited a moment and then put the boot in. The door flew open and, steadying himself against the walls, Terry lurched into the front room.

No one was around, but he spotted the record-player and put on one of his discs which inappropriately declared, "You must have charm".

He staggered into the kitchen and found a carving knife. Holding it in one hand, he picked up the kitchen chairs and hurled them at the dresser.

Then two figures appeared, Edna and Ronnie Carroll. Terry pointed the knife at Ronnie's stomach and said, "I'll give you just ten seconds to explain why you're here."

Then he went over to the record player and turned up the volume saying it would stifle the noise when he killed them both.

His alcohol-befuddled brain was convinced that Edna was going to marry Ronnie and he was determined that if he couldn't marry her, nobody would.

Ronnie was magnificent. "Why don't you grow up," he said in his soft Irish brogue. "You'll never get a woman, behaving like this."

Without a hint of nerves, he turned his back on Terry as if to dare him to try and stab him, and turned down the volume of the record player.

Edna screamed, thinking this was the end of Ronnie.

Terry stood there, not knowing quite what to do.

Then Ronnie turned around and began to walk slowly towards him, his hand outstretched to take the knife.

That did it. All the hate suddenly drained out of Terry. The knife slipped from his hand and dropped to the carpet.

Then Ronnie walked calmly from the room, leaving the pair together. Terry paused, then raced after him shouting, "You're no good if you leave her here with me. You're no good ..."

But Ronnie just kept walking.

Back in the room Terry said to Edna, "Funny him walking out on you like that. He can't think much of you."

Soon he was back to his old charming self and Edna went into the kitchen to make coffee, which they drank cosily sitting on the lounge floor together.

"Terry changed just like that," recalled Edna. "It was as if he didn't remember what had happened. We sat there for ages on the carpet exchanging small talk like a couple of lovesick teenagers."

It was a hard life for Edna. One moment Terry was pleading with her to marry him, the next moment, he didn't care.

Another proposal came after they went to see the film *The Ten Commandments*. Terry suddenly jumped up in the cinema and in front of everyone shouted, "I'm not going to marry you, I don't want you."

And with that he marched out, leaving Edna alone and tearful.

He turned up for the evening show as if nothing had happened, and soon afterwards lounged into her dressing-room at the Finsbury Park Empire and said: "Let's get married."

She followed her cue perfectly. "Shall we?" she said casually.

"Yea," he drawled.

And as simply and as quickly as that, Edna Savage committed herself to becoming Mrs. Terry Dene.

The old Terry Dene in action

A nervous looking Terry clutches his new wife Edna as press photographers fight for vantage points, outside Marylebone Town Hall

Army days. Eating dinner surrounded by reporters

Terry receives his bedding from the Quatermaster's stores

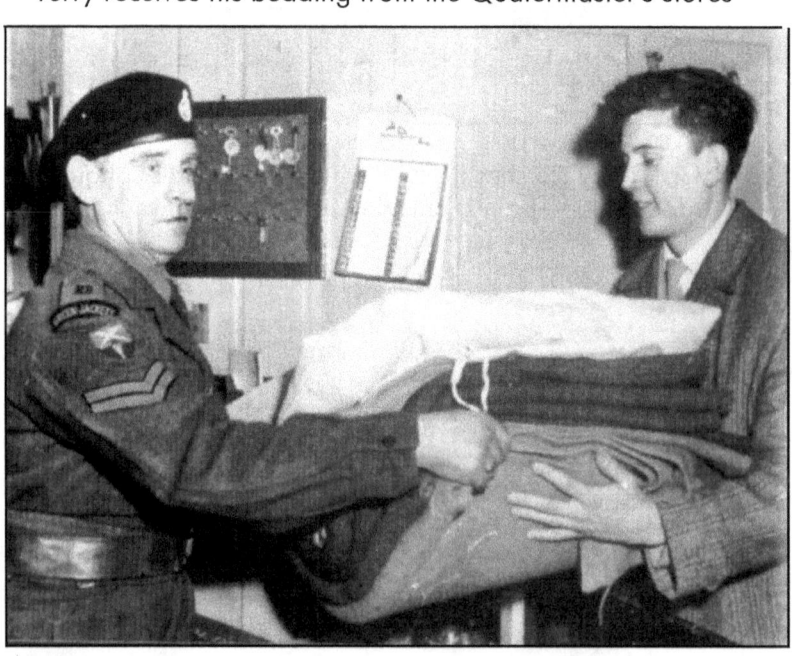

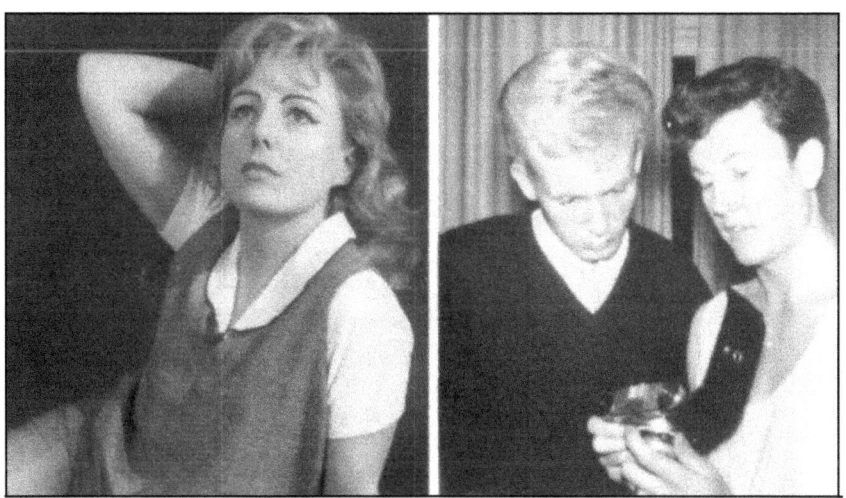

Terry's 'Golden Girl'   Terry with Brian Gregg

Terry, Johnny Gentle, and Billy Fury

Older and Wiser, Terry in Salvation Army uniform during a visit to the Camberwell Corps in London, close to his parents high-rise home

Terry Dene with the *Advocates* during a British tour (1973)

The Mobile Evangelistic Church Crusade mini van in which Terry Dene made his decision to follow Christ

Shortly after his conversion, with some members of the
Mobile Evangelistic Crusade
Far left is Ron Howe, Far Right is Ron Mulcah

Terry plays in the park in Krilbo, Sweden, with his daughter Eve Marie-Louise and wife Margaretta (1972)

The New Terry Dene

Chapter 13

"Pop Girl says 'Yes' to Rock Boy" was how the *Daily Mirror* headlined Edna's decision to marry Terry.

"Terry Dene, £500 a week singing problem of Rock 'n' Roll, popped the question last night to blonde pop singer Edna Savage. And Edna, 22, who got a black eye when 19-year-old Terry went berserk in her hotel at Gloucester four months ago, said 'Yes'.

"It was just before last night's show at the Finsbury Park Empire that Terry asked Edna to marry him. He said later that before popping the question he had discussed it with his psychiatrist. Terry added: 'He thought it would be a good idea for me to marry and settle down'.

"As Edna was on stage – singing 'All the Way' and 'Who's Sorry Now?' – Terry talked in his dressing room of their wedding plans. 'I have been thinking about if for some now, he said. 'Edna and I have been touring together for the past eight weeks. Tonight I made up my mind to ask her be my wife. It was all very sudden. But she accepted immediately.' The wedding day? Terry said, 'We are going to be married in a register office in London on July 8th. Then we plan to go to the South of Spain for ten days' honeymoon'."

The wedding was on, but Terry's psychiatrist was, in fact, completely opposed to it. "What makes you think you can get married?" he asked Terry when he heard the news. "With respect, how on earth can you look after someone else when you cannot look after yourself? If you get married, I shall wash my hands of you."

Terry ignored him. Edna had said "Yes" and he was going ahead with the plans whatever anyone else said.

Edna told me: "I suppose I said I would marry him because so many people had advised me against it. I wanted to prove them wrong. If they had left me alone the whole story could have been different. Terry's father told me not to marry Terry. He said he was unstable."

The big day came – July 8th, 1958 – and Marylebone Register Office, London, was besieged by screaming fans, who fought for a glimpse of the couple.

TERRY DENE: BRITAIN'S FIRST ROCK AND ROLL REBEL

The *London Star* described it as "the wedding of the ex-£4-a-week packer and the ex-£4-a-week telephonist". Terry, wearing a dark grey suit with double pin stripe, narrow trousers with no turn-ups, a white silk tie threaded with gold lamé, and a white carnation, arrived half an hour early. Much to Edna's disgust, his hair was trimmed to semi-crew-cut length and perfumed.

Teenage girls crowded the doorway as the diminutive Edna arrived wearing a tight-waisted, full-skirted short white dress with short sleeves, high neck and decorated by three bows, a platter hat smothered with lily of the valley and a corsage of pink orchids. She had short white gloves and white sandals, with stiletto heels to bring her 5 ft 1 in a little closer to Terry's 5 ft 9 ins.

Terry looked far more at ease than Edna. She was pale and told waiting newsmen: "I feel terrible." Best man was Wee Willie Harris, the wild raving rock 'n' roll singer and comedian, dressed in 35 guineas' worth of full morning dress. "Poor Willie," said Terry when we talked about the day, "he had dyed his hair orange and because of the heat the dye was dripping down his face. He looked quite a sight!"

Harris, minus his usual polka-dot bow tie, baggy candy-striped suit and neon shoes, told a reporter: "I think it is good for Terry to get married – sort of settles him down. But it's not for me, chum."

They left the register office for a service of blessing at the Church of the Annunciation near Great Cumberland Place.

Terry described the scene outside the register office in *The People*: "A shrilling mob of fans fought for vantage places with Press photographers. A battery of agents – you could tell them by the battery of fountain pens in their breast pockets – stood strong and true outside the door.

"With a send-off like that I suppose Edna and I had about a much chance of life-long happiness as a snowflake in the Congo."

Looking back, both Terry and Edna said they could sense disaster ahead, but at that stage they put on a brave face – after all, the show must go on.

That night they booked into a hotel near Edna's flat, and they were horrified to find they had been given twin beds. But Terry hadn't the nerve to ask for something cosier, and they couldn't stay at Edna's flat because it was packed with relatives who had come for the wedding.

"Let's go to the pictures," suggested a nervous Terry, sitting on one of the narrow beds. "It'll take our minds off things."

"O.K., why not?" answered the blushing bride.

So the newly-weds strolled through the West End – straight into a bevy of cameramen and a crowd of star-spotters. Not realising what was going on, they walked into a cinema, only to be greeted by the glare of scores of flashlights.

"By mistake, we had walked into the premier of *The Vikings*," Edna told me. "The next day we captured the headlines – much to the disgust of the other personalities who had gone along especially to be noticed that night!"

The first night of the honeymoon went quietly, to say the least. Both were soon soundly snoring. Next morning Edna woke first with a splitting headache. She looked at her sleeping husband and wondered what lay ahead for them.

Lincoln went to see the couple before they flew for Gibraltar next day for a short stay. "Edna looked really shaky and when Terry was out of the room, she kept repeating: 'What have I done?'" he said.

When they arrived in Gibraltar, it was twin beds again.

In Spain they escaped the cameramen, raced along the 90-mile stretch of coast road to Torremolinos in a hired car and went straight onto the beach. The sun was shining; the sea was blue and they began to feel better. So they stayed right there on the beach, toasting themselves. By evening they were roasted – so frizzled and red that they couldn't even bear the sheets on their bodies.

Despite the sunburn, Edna decided to play the dutiful wife, and put on a sexy, long-flowing white négligée. But Terry wasn't in the mood. "I don't want to be married to you. Who wants you?" he rasped, and stormed out of the bridal suite. He wandered moodily around the streets of Torremolinos full of anger because he had again walked straight down a blind alley. He should never have got married, he told himself.

When he returned, Edna suggested they should get the marriage annulled.

He ignored the idea for a moment and stood admiring himself in the mirror, muttering "Aren't I good looking? Much better than you. Annulled? Sounds like a good idea." The marriage still hadn't been consummated, and a divorce seemed the answer. But they decided to keep up the pretence a little longer, desperately hoping that things might improve.

By the fourth day, relations were just as bad and Terry was working himself up into a terrible state. So he did the sensible thing and rang his psychiatrist in England, who agreed to talk to him. In fact it was the other way round, and Terry raved on and on. The call cost a small fortune, but Terry felt better afterwards and slept well that night – on his own.

Next morning, Edna said suspiciously: "Who were you on the phone to so late last night?"

"My psychiatrist," he replied.

She gave him a sad look. "Perhaps we had better forget this honeymoon," she said.

Terry saw her point and they returned to London six days earlier than intended, fed up, peeling from their day on the beach and smarting from the disastrous non-start to their marriage.

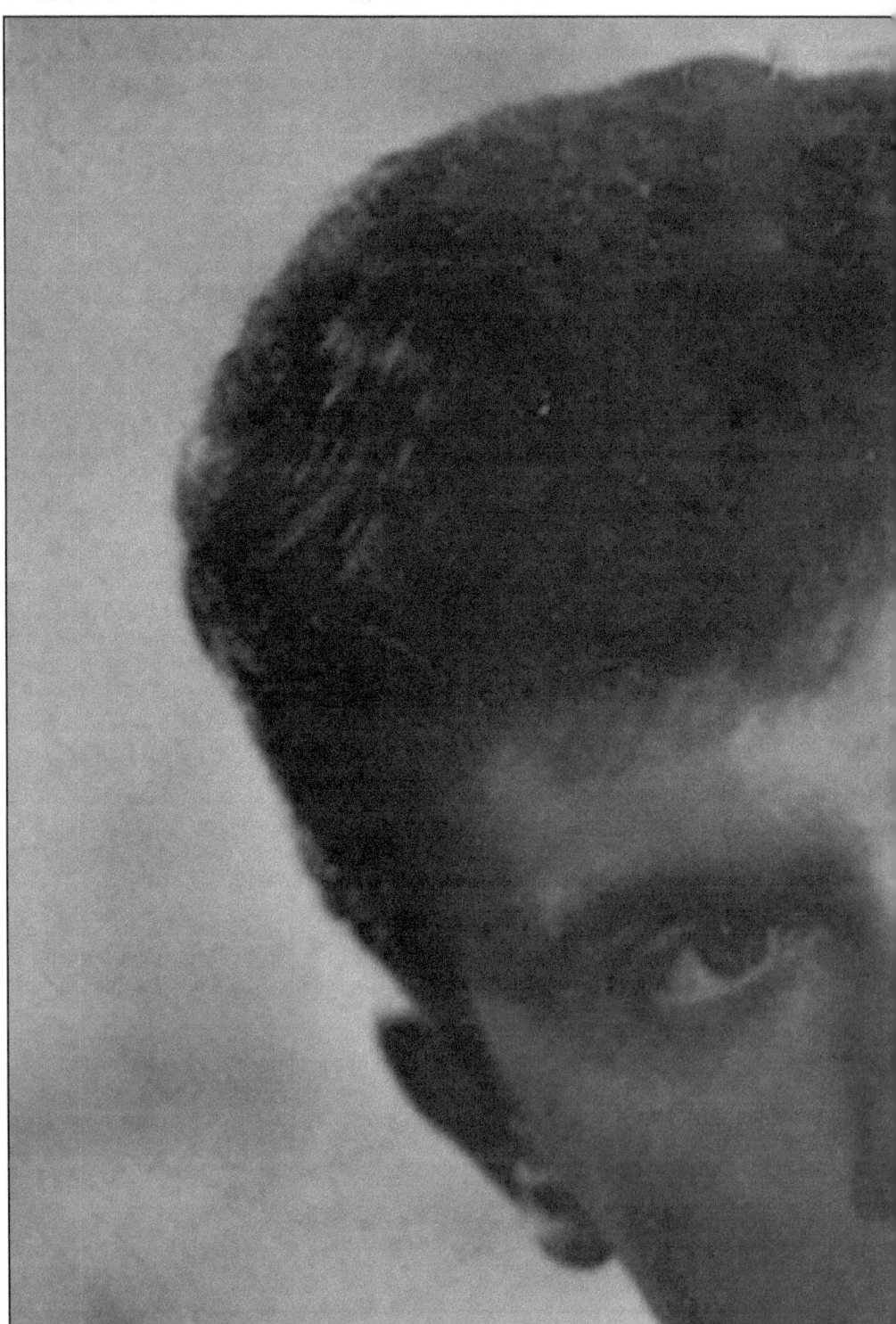

Chapter 14

The marriage was to limp on for some time yet. For Terry, it was a time of intense confusion. One moment he loved his pretty, talented wife, and the next he couldn't bear to be with her.

So he decided to buy a bicycle, although he had a car, and do some visiting of relatives. He also brought a track suit and his mind whirled as his legs pounded the pedals. While he clocked up the miles he desperately tried to work out what had gone wrong, with him, and his marriage.

Edna was booked in Rhyl, North Wales, for a week and Terry hadn't seen her for six days. Surely there must be a way to salvage their 21-day marriage. Eventually he came up with a theory which he was sure would solve everything. He went to a call box and phoned a worried Edna in North Wales.

"Hello, Edna. It's your husband speaking," he began.

"Terry Dene, what are you playing at? Where are you?" she snapped.

"I'm off to visit an aunt and I've been to see Hymie. Hope the show is going well. Look, I know what's wrong with us. Our trouble is that we never do anything ordinary like most couples. You will be back soon and then we will have to start doing some ordinary things. Yes, that's the answer."

The phone clicked and went dead and Terry headed for his aunt's, leaving Edna wondering what he would do next.

"That day life seemed so unreal," she told me.

Terry began his "ordinary" life by painting the flat; he soon lost interest and his theory was shattered, but he came up with another idea.

"Let's go to Paris and get away from the telephone. We'll have a ball over there. It's just what we need."

A friend of a friend knew Brigitte Bardot and maybe they could get to meet her.

A confused Edna dutifully packed a couple of cases and, leaving their partly painted flat, they headed for Heathrow to catch a flight to Paris. Edna was a fan of the sexy and glamorous Bardot and thought the meeting would be a never-to-be-forgotten experience.

They checked into a swish hotel and Terry raved about the fabulous time they would have.

But as Edna sat making herself up for their first evening, Terry changed. In the mirror she watched his face cloud and his eyes glaze. "I don't want to go out in Paris with you. I'm going out on my own," he shouted.

"But Terry, I thought we would go together," she said desperately.

"I don't care what I said. I don't want to go out with you. You can stay here and wait for me."

He emptied her handbag onto the bed, pocketed her passport and money and stormed out, slamming the door behind him.

Shaken, Edna sat on the edge of the bed, fighting back the tears. She finally lay down wondering what Terry would do next. She dozed fitfully until her drunken husband staggered into the room.

"Terry, it's six in the morning. What you have been up to?"

"None of your business," his drunken voice said.

"Terry, I want my passport and money back."

He hurled the passport at her. "You can't have your money back. It's all gone. I've had it stolen. Oooh, my head. I feel awful."

With that he collapsed on the bed and was soon snoring loudly. She shook him, "What do you mean, you've had it stolen?"

"Shut up, Edna, can't you see I'm not well?"

Desperately she searched his pockets, but there was no cash. They were staying at an expensive hotel without money. She phoned a friend in London. "Look, Terry's done it again. He's landed us in a terrible spot. We've got no money." Her friend arranged for a contact in Paris to let them have a loan, which got them back to London. Terry re-acquired his love for painting and soon one wall of the flat had a new Terry Dene gloss. But only one wall, because he became bored. So he pulled the telephone from the wall, much to Edna's annoyance, and stormed out.

Edna still loved Terry and, despite his erratic behaviour, was frantically trying to salvage something from the mess. It was hard going, though, as I learned when we talked at her home.

"One of Terry's big failings was that he loved buying outrageous clothes. He would disappear for hours on end and return dressed in a completely different outfit. Most of the gear he bought was dreadful.

"A lot of my friends wouldn't believe what he was like when I told them. They thought I was exaggerating when I described his antics. One of these doubters was an actor who came round to meet Terry one day and was very impressed. Terry was on his best behaviour for a change and my actor friend told me he thought he was very sweet.

"Terry decided to go out for a while and when he returned a little later he was a different person in more ways than one. As usual, he was completely kitted out in the most way-out gear you have seen, check trousers and shirt. He had left in a conservative suit and my friend was horrified by the transformation. He was obviously in a state of shock and as he went out he stammered 'Oh my dear, Oh my dear'. I heard him repeat this over and over as he left my flat, never to return."

Incidents like that were humorous, said Edna, looking back, but others were quite terrifying.

"Once Terry told his psychiatrist he was afraid he would murder someone and he was advised to go into a clinic. He agreed to sleep there each night and then spend the day with me. I went along to make sure he was all right on the first night. I tucked him in bed like a little child, kissed him, and said 'Goodnight, Terry, don't worry. Everything will be all right.' I breathed a sigh of relief, knowing he was now in safe hands and couldn't do any harm, to me or anyone else.

"When I got back to my flat, guess who was there to greet me? Yes, the one and only Terry Dene. He had run all the way back from the clinic in his pyjamas. He told me he had decided to stay at home with me after all and had just taken off from the clinic. What a man!"

Terry would be the first to admit that in those days he was seriously mentally ill, and not really responsible for his actions. It was a Jekyll and Hyde existence.

"Going to bed at night for me was often horrific," said Edna. "I would be fast asleep and he would wake me up and tell me he had a terrible urge to suffocate me. He would lie awake for hours gazing down at me. I was terrified. It was as if he was controlled by something outside himself.

"I remember the first time he stayed at my mother's home in Warrington. He was in one of these moods and in the night he woke up my mother and told her: 'I can't sleep with your daughter. I'm going to murder her!' She didn't know about his problems and was terrified."

Edna added, "One of the times Terry said he had this urge to kill was when we were staying in a Bristol hotel. He realised he needed help and phoned his psychiatrist, who immediately came down from London. The doctor arranged for another man to be there with us and sleep in the room with Terry, while I stayed in another room.

"Another incident illustrating Terry's cruel streak at that time happened when we were staying at Sheffield where I was appearing in pantomime.

"The landlady was thrilled to have us at her digs. At first Terry was charming to her. She was obviously very impressed. Then he changed when he found she had a cat she loved very much. She had a fear, he discovered, of her cat getting out onto the road and being killed. He cottoned on to this.

"One day he came in and told her he had just seen a cat killed in the road. 'Is it yours?' he asked. She went white. In fact Terry hadn't seen any such thing. He just wanted to upset the woman." Even so, there were warm moments between the couple and the marriage was finally consummated. But that went wrong too – Edna's pregnancy had to be terminated by a major operation.

Then, to add to their problems, Terry was called up. Those were the days of National Service, and Edna, knowing his mental state, saw big trouble ahead. So did his psychiatrist, who issued a report to the Army saying Terry was definitely not fit to join up.

But the Army had other ideas. They had decided to use the rock 'n' roll star for a massive publicity campaign.

A close friend of Terry's told me, "The Army decided to cash in on Elvis's call-up and mount a British publicity campaign like the Americans had used for Presley. They printed posters with slogans like 'Terry's joined, how about you?'

"I'm sure they got the psychiatrist's report on him, but ignored it, hoping he would be O.K. After all, they were bound to win a lot of friends and recruits from the publicity."

As the start of the two years of National Service grew nearer, Terry tried to reconcile himself to no longer being an entertainer, just plain 23604106 Rifleman Williams. He was to join the Greenjackets at Winchester; in some ways he looked forward to a fresh start and returning to being an ordinary guy again.

It might have gone better if he had been left alone to do just that, but the Press wouldn't hear of it. Terry was always good copy and his call-up was a great story.

Edna came through her operation but was still feeling groggy the week before he joined up.

Terry was asked if he would mind going to the camp at Winchester for a Press preview. He turned the request down flat, but unfortunately that was not the end of it. Hymie was for it, so was the Army, and the papers were screaming for preview pictures.

And so, against his better judgement, Terry agreed to go. At the camp, the preview was all laid on. The Army was co-operating up to the hilt – at least the Top Brass were.

The lads had a very different attitude. While Terry was having his hair cut and lining up for grub at the canteen, with pictures being shot from all angles, the boys in khaki showed their feelings in no uncertain manner.

"Mummy's darling!" yelled one.

"Just wait until next week!" and "Get him!" came in quick succession.

All the cameramen would say was "Take no notice, Terry. Just smile! This way – smile!"

Jack Bentley, writing in the *Daily Mirror,* called Terry's visit to Winchester "an astonishing preview".

"I was with him when he called at what will be his first Army 'home' – Winchester Barracks – to ask if he could be shown round and meet his future companions," he wrote. "After waiting in the guardroom, where Terry was asked for his autograph by a regimental policeman, we were ushered into the Adjutant's office.

There, Captain P.E. Willis-Fleming proved to be not a bit warlike. He gave Terry permission to preview the lot. The Adjutant shook hands with Terry and told him that the King's Royal Rifles were all ready to welcome him for the start of his two years' National Service. RSM J. Pope confirmed this with another handshake.

"Under escort we moved on to regimental barber Pennycook, who is a Terry Dene fan. But fan or no fan, he told Terry that this week those famous Dene locks would be lopped off – and no nonsense.

"On to the canteen. Here Terry lined up with a couple of lads from his own part of London – Riflemen F.R. Reade and B. Carter. We were all served by starry-eyed NAAFI girl Janice Hurn. In the corner of the canteen was a juke box. But Terry's name wasn't on the list of records.

"Said Terry, 'It's just as well, because if I've got to take a break away from rock 'n' roll, it might as well be a clean one.' And to prove it, he isn't even taking his guitar to Winchester. He has sold his luxury sports car and will arrive at the gates in an Army lorry with the 40 other National Servicemen."

Terry was whisked back to London to do a television spot for Jack Jackson – in uniform. He felt resentful and angry at the way he had been manipulated, and not a little uneasy at the reaction of the other soldiers. He decided to phone Edna from the studio.

She was in Sheffield at the Empire Theatre with Laurie London, who had a hit with "He's Got the Whole World In His Hand", and then, like so many in the fifties, disappeared from the limelight.

The call ended with a row and Edna saying firmly, "It's no good, Terry. I can't take any more. I'm going to divorce you. Our marriage, if you can call it that, is over."

Terry had brightly told her he was back with an old girl friend and couldn't comprehend why Edna was angry. He went wild, pulling the telephone out of the wall, breaking a chair and screaming and shouting.

Luckily his father was with him. "Snap out of it; you've got a show to do," he told him.

"But Edna's going to divorce me," he said.

"Worry about that later," said his dad. "Get on and do the show."

So he did, somehow. But his last night as Terry Dene was a far from happy one.

Chapter 15

The rock 'n' roll rifleman duly reported for duty the following day, feeling as though he was about to face the firing squad.

And in a very real way he was, for his life was about to be shot to pieces.

At Waterloo Terry left behind a crowd of chanting fans and settled down in his carriage with the other 35-shillings-a-week servicemen on the draft.

"So you're Terry Dene," said a tough-looking customer next to him in the swaying train. "My bird fancies you. Me, I've never reckoned you."

Terry smiled, but his thoughts were miles away.

"That's your privilege, mate."

Edna's face was constantly in his mind: he couldn't shake off the vision.

At Winchester station, the group climbed into a lorry, which bumped along uncomfortably to the camp gates.

"Wow, look at that reception," said the touch customer, eyeing the crowds of teenagers, Pressmen and Army brass at the gates. "I'll give it you, Dene, you must have something to attract that lot."

Teenagers whistled and screamed as he popped his face out of the back of the lorry and waved, and there were shouts of "Good luck, Terry!"

The screaming reached fever pitch as he clambered out of the back of the Army lorry; immediately the photographers and newsreel men took over, and Terry had to pose for numerous pictures. Several times he strode backwards and forwards through the barrack gate; then a Press officer suggested that the media men should adjourn to the mess and shoot movie pictures.

They clamoured for vantage points as Terry collected his pie and mash and sat down at a table. Almost before he had finished his meal, he was rushed to the quartermaster's stores to be kitted out. "Just one more shot, Terry!" "Could you do it again?"

It was sheer hell for Terry. It was all too obvious that the other recruits resented him, and the boys who had been there some time were making cracks under their breath so the officers couldn't hear. But Terry could: his worst fears were confirmed.

Finally he turned to an officer. "Sir, when are the Press men going?"

"Don't worry," he said. "They'll be off soon."

Terry knew the Press. "I'd appreciate it if they'd go soon, sir. All this is causing bad feeling."

But they stayed. The circus trooped everywhere after the unwilling star, until at last they decided that Terry had put up with enough.

But the damage was done: in his barrack room Terry had a cool reception, and as he was queuing for breakfast next morning, he heard another recruit say: "That's Terry Dene – he's married to that singer, Edna Savage."

"How does a stupid b--- like him get a girl like that?" his chum retorted. The reaction had set in.

"He was a big star once, but he's all washed up now."

Terry longed to make a run for it, get out of earshot of the cutting remarks – but where could he go? For two long years he was to be a servant of the British Army: and it seemed that all that was worst in show business was to follow him even there: they would persuade him, use him and, when their purpose had been served, discard him. And he was fed up with being used.

Sick, lost, desperate, he sat down and tried to write to Edna. Her last words "I'm going to divorce you," kept hammering in his brain. In spite of all the quarrels, he was still madly in love with her.

Suddenly he began to cry.

"What's the matter, Terry?" asked a sympathetic chap in the barrack room.

"I don't know," was all he could say. "I just don't know."

He was sobbing uncontrollably and a puzzled corporal helped him to another room. He sat there in his thick itchy khaki trying to tell him how he was feeling.

All the corporal could suggest was a trip to the Medical Officer. "You're not much good to the Army like this," he told him.

Those words were to have shattering consequences for Terry Dene. They led to the eventual end of his career, questions in the House of Commons, and a campaign of hate unprecedented in British show business history.

His pre-Army antics like breaking windows and being drunk and disorderly never really did him much harm with the public. But his breakdown as a soldier was to ruin him.

In the morning, an Army doctor gave Terry an icy look. "Elvis Presley did it," he said sternly. "Why can't you?"

Terry was desperate. "Have you seen the reports on my mental condition?" he asked. "Did you know that psychiatrists' reports about me have been sent in by three individual doctors?"

Surprise registered on the doctor's face. He went out of the room.

Terry sat there for 30 minutes, his despair deepening every moment. When the doctor returned, his attitude was quite different.

"Don't worry," he said gently. "Everything's going to be all right."

A sergeant was brought in and Terry was told he was being taken to Netley Army Hospital. As they wheeled out he whispered to Terry, "Don't worry about this, boy. At least five of the lads who came in with you won't make it either."

His face flushed slightly as he added: "By the way, can I have your autograph?"

At Netley, Terry went out like a light. He slept for three days solid, coming up only for the occasional mouthful of food.

The Press were soon on his trail again, but this time it was a different story – because the Army did a rapid about-turn. They no longer wanted any publicity on Terry Dene. Like the man said, he was of no use to them in that condition.

"TWO-DAY SOLDIER TERRY DENE GOES SICK," said the headlines. The rocking rifleman was splash news throughout the nation, and radio and television bulletins were full of the story.

And it wasn't just Terry who suffered. His parents heard at first hand what the Army thought of their son. As they stood in a milk-bar waiting for their train after a visit to Netley, a veteran sergeant roared: "I've heard just about enough of Terry Dene and his troubles. Look at the money he's made. The Army will do him the world of good."

Mrs. Williams, already upset by seeing Terry, jumped up. "You don't know what you're talking about. You're fit and he's not. I ought to know, I'm his mum," she shouted pathetically.

The embarrassed sergeant apologised.

After a fortnight at Netley, the Army doctors were still not sure that Terry was fit for discharge, so they bundled him off to a civilian mental hospital near Epsom, Surrey.

It was too much for Terry. In his new ward he threw himself down on the bed and sobbed. But as the days went by he found it wasn't so bad after all. He was surrounded by all sorts of mixed-up characters: alcoholics, drug addicts, and men whose marriages had foundered, causing them to founder as well. At last, in a world of misfits, Terry fitted in. These were his kind of people. They all had problems – like him – and he wasn't alone with his thoughts any more.

Every morning he was up at seven, cleaning windows, polishing floors, and doing odd jobs. After breakfast he chatted with a psychiatrist, whose questions were mainly about his childhood.

Edna was in a nursing home, recovering from her operation. She had lost a stone and a half in five days. A steady stream of poison pen letters about her "yellow" husband hit her hard and, still feeling groggy, she made her way to see Terry at the Epsom hospital. The taxi fare was £15. She was shocked to see the change in him ... he was pale, shaky and looked 20 years older. "He looked much sadder but no wiser," she told me.

"I like it here," he told Edna as they held hands. "They're a nice bunch of lads though they seem a bit muddled."

Meanwhile, a major storm was brewing over his breakdown.

The Press, as usual, were after information and finding it difficult to get, but a Home Office spokesman did tell one newspaper: "This does NOT mean that he has been discharged. He has been admitted as an Army patient."

Two Army doctors and a top-ranking psychiatrist eventually recommended that Terry should be discharged from the Army as being medically unfit. But the War Office decided not to discharge him – at least for the time being.

Edna started her own campaign to get Terry discharged. She spent hours trying to persuade officials at the War Office that discharge would be the best thing.

"I'm fighting to get you out," she told Terry. "I think I'll win."

His reply was the same as before: "I like it here. I don't want to leave. I feel secure here."

Now newspaper men were falling over themselves to offer large sums of money to get to Terry. "You could take me in as a relative," said one. "I am authorised to pay you several thousand pounds if you will!"

But Edna, for Terry's sake, wouldn't hear of it, although she could have used the money. She was horrified to hear that a friend had accepted a £20 bribe to smuggle a reporter in for an "exclusive" interview.

Then came a shock – an unexpected Easter present. A medical board again recommended a discharge to the War Office on the ground that Terry was "medically unfit for further service". This time the War Office agreed.

A few hours after meeting an Army medical board, Terry had his own suit on – hanging a bit around his waist because he had lost a lot of weight – and was getting on the train for London and Edna.

He was out of the Army; but two new fears faced Terry. How would Edna react to his return, and how would the fans treat an Army reject?

Edna lay asleep in the flat. A hail of pebbles rattled against her window and she woke up to see Terry on the pavement. The doorbell was out of order and he had no key. Of course, he wasn't alone. A group of reporters had virtually camped out on the doorstep throughout Terry's illness.

"Can we come in with him?" asked one of them, holding out a bottle of champagne. "Just for a minute? Please?"

And they all came in.

Edna told a *Daily Mail* man: "I thought the Army would be good for him. But I'm satisfied that if the Army doctors think he should be discharged, then that is the best thing for him." She added: "You'd have thought the Army would have let me know he was coming home. It's Easter and I've hardly got enough food in the flat for us."

They clasped hands and Terry, looking pale and shaky, told them "I'm not through with the treatment; I'm still an out-patient. I've got a lot of psychoanalysis to go through yet.

"Edna and I want to get to know each other all over again. We'd like to take a holiday together in the sun, but we can't go too far away because I have to keep going to the hospital."

But while Terry and Edna were trying to get to know each other again, hostilities broke out between two Ministries and the War Office and a major storm gathered over the discharge of the rock 'n' roll singer.

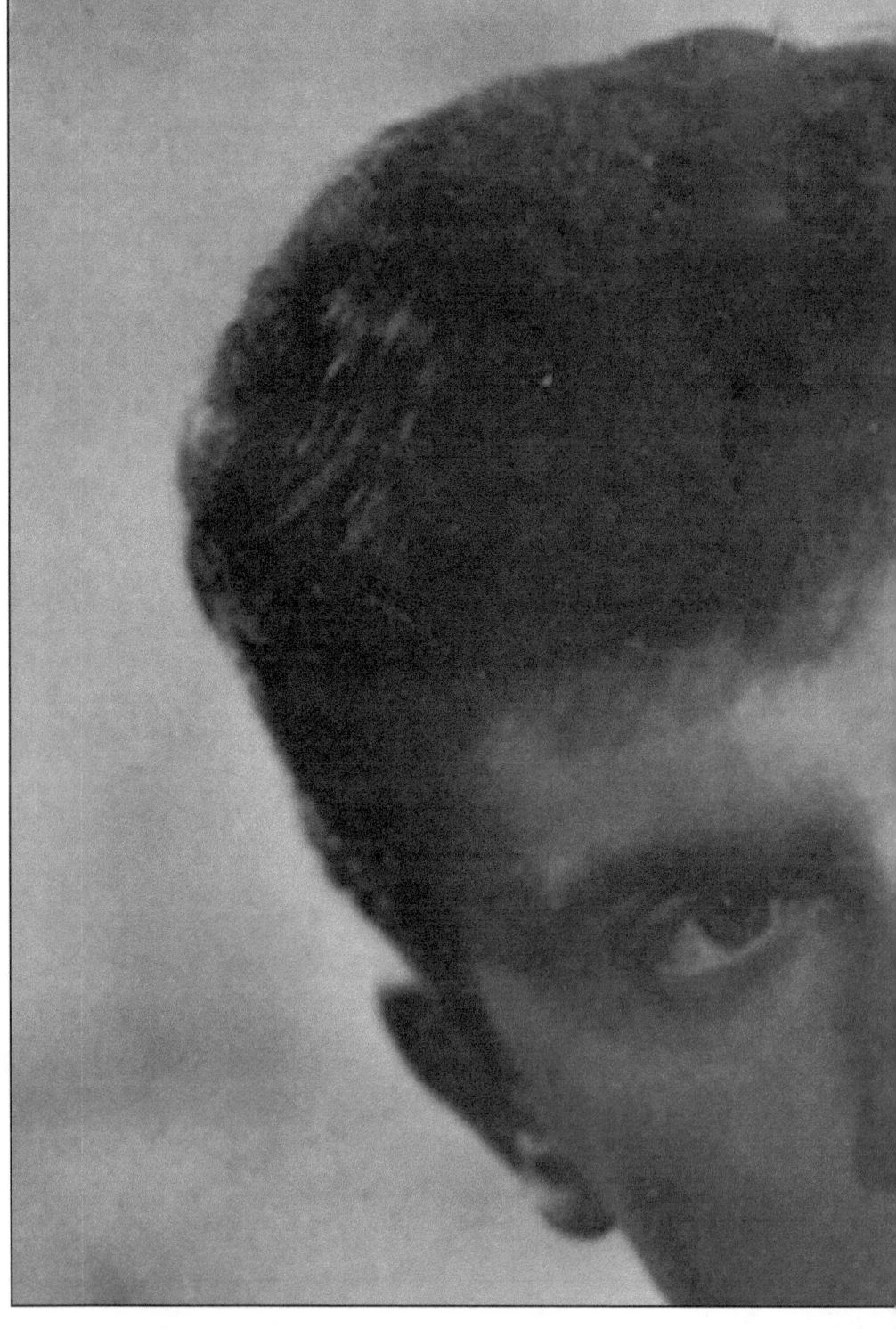

Chapter 16

The Rev. Geoffrey Beaumont stood before his congregation at St. George's Church, Camberwell. "Let us pray for Terry Dene – a young man who has been very ill – and help his path through a rather complicated and eventful time," he said. "Dene's life depends a lot on what happens today."

Terry certainly needed those prayers. That night his comeback was beginning – and now boos, violence and insults mingled with the screams of adulation from his teenage fans.

The first of his series of one-nighters was in Derby, and when he arrived at the Majestic cinema, it was to find the walls plastered with slogans saying "Down with Terry Dene!" The manager told him "I've had a tip-off that lads from the local Army camp are going to be in the audience to make trouble."

He was taking no chances and had prepared for the concert as if the Russians were invading. A strong-arm force of 15 cinema managers mixed with the audience. They were reinforced by five massive Army redcaps, a police sergeant, two constables and a policewoman.

"It's a wonder they had any room for the audience," Terry joked later.

But at the time it was no joke. As he prepared to go on with his old group, the *Dene-aces*, nausea welled up inside him – a product of his desperation for success. He tensed up, taut like the high string on his guitar. He was about to snap, and he knew it.

The booing started as soon as the curtain went up. The 1,000-strong audience loomed in front of him and he tried to gather his senses. The group had already tuned up and plugged in, and as Terry opened his mouth for the first number, a raucous voice from the gallery bellowed: "When's your leave up?" Then someone shouted "Wakey-wakey!"

But the words came out and by the time he was half-way through the song, a group of fans in the stalls began yelling "We want Terry! We want Terry!" They cheered wildly when he finished, and he smiled weakly and pressed on.

His choice of songs could have been better, though. "I'd like to sing one of my favourite songs, 'Poor Boy'," he announced amid the whistles and boos.

It was an open invitation for a soldier in the audience. "You're not poor Dene. You're getting more for this show than we get for months of hard work!"

Terry battled on as the chants got louder, both sides trying to outdo the other.

"Get back to the Army!" "Where's your stretcher?"

"We love you, Terry!"

The 20-minuted spot finished and Terry marched straight off the stage. The theatre was in uproar. As he sat shaking in his tiny dressing room, the rival groups met in the foyer. Girl fans shouted at soldiers and soldiers yelled back at fans. The security people tried to stop fighting breaking out. Meanwhile, for 90 minutes, Terry sat motionless in black misery looking at his pale face in the mirror.

Then a group of redcaps came into the dressing room and hustled him away. "Just stick close, son, and you'll be all right," they told him. "We've got a police car waiting to get you away." He was hustled though a police cordon into the waiting car, which sped away into the night.

Next night the show was at sedate Harrogate in Yorkshire, in front of 1,300 people: again the noise was deafening. Terry was in the middle of a number when the chanting began. This time most of the audience were on his side as they yelled "Down with the Army!" But good fortune was against him: the microphone cut out.

"Bring him back to us," wailed girls in the gallery as electricians worked frantically to bring back the sound – and Dene.

The power soon came on again and the show became a triumph. Terry sang to the noisy backing of his group, shrieks, the rhythmic clapping of hands and shouts of "Good old Terry!"

There were even two young national servicemen in uniform in the audience who said they were from Catterick Camp. They had paid 32½p each for their seats, 14p in fares and would get back to Catterick 10 minutes before their passes expired. They were pro-Dene.

As Terry's one and only night of triumph ended, there was a concerted rush by fans for the two doors leading to the stage. Stewards fought to stop them getting to the dressing-room and, luckily for Terry, succeeded – at least for a time. They would have ripped him apart.

Terry allowed Pressmen into his dressing-room and raved about his reception. Just then a group of girls broke through the stewards' cordon and reached his dressing-room door. They hammered on it. "Come out, Terry! We love you, Terry!"

Terry just sat there and smiled. He'd given everything he'd got, and they had loved it.

It was back to trouble the next night. The hall's manager called him to the phone. "A chap here won't give his name, but he says he wants to talk to you."

Terry picked up the receiver. "Hello, Terry Dene. Can I help you?"

"Sure you can help, Dene. You can help by not going on tonight. I warn you, you go on tonight and you'll be shot. I shall be in the audience and if you dare show your face on stage I shall shoot to kill!" With that the phone went dead, and Terry died a little, too.

"You all right, Mr. Dene?" said the worried manager, as Terry slumped onto a seat. "Like a drink to calm you down?"

"No. I'll be all right in a minute."

Far from being the coward many dubbed him, Terry had tremendous courage. He ignored the death threat and went on. Nothing happened, but it could have done. Terry kept a watchful eye open, but would never have been able to prevent a shooting in the darkened theatre.

Next night he arrived at the stage door with his group in a northern town. They were met by a group of louts.

"Have you seen much of our town?" said the leader to drummer Clem Cattini.

"No."

"Well, you will – in the ambulance on the way to hospital."

With that the friendly northerners shaped up for a fight, but Terry and the *Dene-aces* showed them they were ready and the louts fled.

But the day after, Terry made a fatal mistake; he arrived at another theatre on his own. A group of thugs jumped on him from out of the shadows by the stage door and hustled him to the ground. The boot went in. His body and face resounded with sickening thuds; he lay helplessly on the floor as they vented all their hatred for the rock 'n' roll "coward".

At last, satisfied they had taught Dene a lesson; they left him semi-conscious on the ground and ran off.

Terry managed to drag himself up and into the theatre, his battered face looking like a side of beef and his senses swimming in a red mist. He staggered into the dressing-room and the Dene-aces' welcome turned to outrage as they saw what had happened. "Who did that?" said Clem. "Tell me, Terry, and we'll go and sort them out."

Terry could hardly speak, so Clem raced outside; but the thugs were long gone. As the others went to follow Clem, Terry, his face swollen, whispered "Leave them; if they are so unintelligent they want to beat people up, they're just not worth bothering with." The screaming and jeering audience that night never saw through Terry's heavy make-up.

He gave a fine performance.

As the group's van pulled up for the next date at a ballroom, another gang of youths was there to greet them. Some of the group made it obvious they had armed themselves with a crowbar and the thugs took the hint. But the gang got their revenge, for as the Dene-aces' hired van was pulling away after the show, they kicked the back. They hacked away till the driver jammed on the brakes. In a blazing temper he went round the back, and screamed "Who did that?"

The gang stood there in silence. "Why don't you idiots grow up?" he stormed. "Oh, I give up!"

With that he stomped back to the driver's seat, hardly believing that people could be so vicious over a man being discharged from the Army.

The tour limped on its stormy way. Another night Terry needed extra strong protection, for some of the trouble-makers in the audience decided they were going to teach him a lesson.

A group of burly bouncers escorted him to the rear exit. One thug took a swing at Terry, but instead hit a bouncer. Terry ran for his life and dived into the back of the van. Stones hurtled all around. He lay there, hardly daring to breathe, while the louts searched for him. They eventually gave up and went home.

For those eight nights, Terry picked up £400, and out of that he had to pay £130 to his musicians. Not much for a comeback that he only just survived.

Chapter 17

As Terry was supposedly rocking and rolling his way back to a "fortune", the storm surrounding his discharge gathered momentum.

The Ministry of Defence blamed the War Office for "undesirable publicity", unlikely to help its aim of boosting the Army as a worthwhile career.

The War Office was wondering why the Ministry of Defence called up Dene in the first place.

The Ministry of Labour, like the Defence men, was annoyed about the publicity.

Thousands said openly that he had been given "celebrity treatment", that he had fiddled his discharge, that he was swinging the lead.

In Parliament, too, there were many who, to say the least found it difficult to reconcile his illness with the speed of his comeback.

Gerald Nabarro, for example, voiced his suspicion that there was one law for normal National Servicemen and another for the "stars". He was backed by a Nottingham M.P., who commented, "The rejection for the Forces or immediate release on medical grounds of these people earning big money, whether they be T.V. stars, racing drivers or first-class cricketers who score a century within a week of being refused on medical grounds, causes great resentment." For Terry was not the only object of Mr. Nabarro's wrath: Marty Wilde and Colin Cowdrey had also been found unfit for military service.

"There's really no excuse at all," he protested. "Just because they can earn large sums of money in civilian life or are prominent sportsmen - the overwhelming majority of young men have to do their full two years."

An angry Christopher Soames hit back, pointing out that an average of 1% of recruits were found at a later stage to be medically unfit. He added: "I must absolutely refute the inference cast by you as to the attitude adopted by the medical authorities." Many others flocked to their defence too, including the *Daily Telegraph* medical consultant.

"How worthwhile it is training an unsuitable candidate or one likely to break down physically or mentally," he wrote, "can only be answered by competent medical authorities, often with more knowledge than is publicly revealed. All my experience has been that they act scrupulously and honestly on behalf of the Services by whom they are employed."

Iain Macleod, too, affirmed his confidence in the skill and judgement of the medical boards, pointing out that wherever there was doubt, specialists were consulted and anyone feeling hard done by was entitled to appeal.

It was also pointed out that Terry had been sent not only to a military hospital but also to a civil mental hospital, and that both reported him unfit for service.

But Gerald Nabarro, among others, was still not convinced.

"This man did one day's soldiering after being found completely fit for the Army. Within hours of his discharge he is rocking and rolling on television and again earning large sums of money. This case merits further scrutiny," he insisted.

"If it is a psychiatric case, which this seems to have been," replied Mr. Hugh Fraser, "circumstances change swiftly. The final evidence we have is of the civilian and military doctors, to the effect that he was unfit to be a soldier." To which Emmanuel Shinwell, amid laughter, retorted, "Does all this mean that there is plenty of room, on the stage, the music hall and television for psychiatric cases?"

Mr. Fraser tried to explain.

"Apart from mental diseases and psychoneuroses, there are so-called character disorders which people get hot under the collar about. Those suffering from these behave in an erratic way.

"They may occasionally be incapable of ordinary, prudent, sensible behaviour, and are always getting into trouble.

"Many criminals fall into this category.

"A lot of these people are unfit for military service. The degree to which you can discipline people is limited by their characters.

"Criticism that people are 'getting out of military service' is all very well if that is the only way you look at it. But if you want efficient soldiers and do not want to waste time and public money on people who will never be any good as soldiers, it is obviously right to reject them.

"The whole aim, surely, is to create an efficient fighting force, not to run a reform school or an establishment for misfits."

And so the issue was played backwards and forwards in the House of Commons. Some few MPs showed genuine concern for the "misfit" at the centre of it all: for others it was merely another subject for debate and rhetoric; and there were always the few for whom the freedom of the House meant the opportunity to make statements so ill-founded and insensitive that anywhere else they would have been summonsed for slander.

Terry kept quiet in public about the Commons rows; but Edna hit out. "If these people in Parliament would leave variety acts to those who are paid for them and try to do what they're supposed to do, the world might be a better place," she exploded to a *Daily Express* reporter.

"As comedians, they do something we never do in the theatre - pick on a sick man."

Chapter 18

Hymie Zahl sounded agitated as he spoke over the phone to Paul Lincoln.

"I can't take any more of Terry Dene," he said. "This boy's ruining me. I am prepared to give him his contract back. What do you think?" "If that's how you feel, Hymie, let's call it a day. Let's give him his contract back."

Hymie's voice calmed. "Come round to my office and we'll sort it out," he said.

So Paul visited his myopic colleague and was handed a document which, Hymie said, would solve everything. Without examining it Paul signed, thankful he would no longer have to manage the unmanageable singer.

Feeling very pleased with himself, Lincoln handed Hymie the paper. Suddenly, the phone rang and to his amazement Zahl began negotiating a deal on Terry's behalf.

"Yes, that's right," he told the impresario, "I now have sole control over Terry Dene."

Lincoln exploded. "Hymie, you've taken me to the cleaners. You've turned me over," he screamed.

Zahl peered at him and said nothing, his chubby hand cupped over the receiver.

"Hymie, I trusted you ... " Lincoln yelled; then, speechless, he stormed from the room, resolving never again to get involved with the music business.

Shortly afterwards, he was offered the chance to manage a singer who is now one of the biggest names in the business, but he was so shattered by his experiences with Zahl and Terry, that he refused, and threw away a fortune.

Instead, Lincoln went back to the wrestling ring, where he did become famous in an anonymous sort of way - as the terrifying masked Dr. Death. His insight into show business had taught him how to sell a gimmick, and he became a grunt and groan star. Anyone who could beat him could remove his mask - but of course they never did!

Hymie got Terry a two-week run in a Manchester night spot. As work was getting harder and harder to come by, Terry jumped at the chance and persuaded his group to join him.

By now they were getting fed up with the ceaseless controversy and hassle, and were looking for other work, but as a favour to Terry they agreed to play for him this time.

Clem Cattini, in fact, sacrificed a chance to join The Shadows by playing for Terry for that fortnight. Jet Harris had told him to hang around in London as there might be an opening for a drummer in the group very soon. There was, while he was away, and Tony Meehan got the job instead.

After Manchester came the slump. Jobs were even harder to get. Nobody wanted Terry Dene, the boy who seemed to attract trouble wherever he went.

Then Hymie came up with the bright idea of trying Terry abroad. "I've got a nice little fortnight booked for you in Sweden, Terry," he bubbled. "It's just what you need."

Terry wasn't too happy, especially as Edna had got a booking which made it impossible for her to go. There was just himself, bass guitarist Brian Gregg, and drummer Clem. Terry had made a previous visit to Stockholm to promote *The Golden Disc* and that had been a big success, so many of his fans came for a second look at their idol - but by now it was a different idol they saw.

At nights before they went on Terry used to think of Edna and all the chances he had messed up. He began drinking again. Most of the time he didn't let the booze interfere with him too much, and managed to get on stage and go through his routine in the polished Dene manner, but really he was like a robot.

Then, almost inevitably as it seemed, he blew his chance again. Just an hour before he was due on stage he went back to his hotel - loaded to the gills - and packed a suitcase. He rang the air terminal and asked an English – speaking clerk the "time of the next plane to Edna".

"To Edna?" the poor clerk queried.

"Don't argue with me," Terry told him. "To London then!"

There wasn't a plane until the next day, but in his drunken miserable state he called a cab and told the driver to take him to the airport.

Halfway there he stopped the cabby, paid him off and sat at the roadside on his suitcase trying to puzzle out through the haze of drink what he was doing.

The crisp Swedish air was clearing his head a little, and he began to realise that if the news got back to London that he had walked out on the show he would really be finished – for good.

Back at the theatre the audience was waiting for the show to start. The group was on stage, instruments at the ready, hoping and praying that Terry would make a last-minute appearance.

The curtains went up, the audience clapped and cheered. There was a pregnant pause and then Clem hissed to Brian: "Sing, man, sing."

So he did. He swung his hips like Terry and launched into "Whole lotta shakin' going on". He did the whole show himself, and was quite a hit!

Backstage, Hymie was going mad. "He's ruined me," he screamed. "That boy has ruined me this time. What shall I do?"

"I shall never book another English artist again," yelled the Swedish impresario. "Never again, Mr. Zahl."

The news of Terry's latest escapade was soon flashed to London and spread like wildfire. A tour of Britain with Edna and Terry as the big names was immediately cancelled.

Terry struggled back to his hotel, now comprehending what he had done. He wanted to scream. What made him do such stupid things?

"Edna," said a subdued Hymie as he phoned from Stockholm. "Edna, my dear, you must talk to him. He's gone and done it again. He's ruining me."

"Put him on," said a weary Edna.

"Hello, Edna, it's Terry here," he said brightly.

"Terry," she said angrily. "This time I'm through. And I mean it."

"Divorce? No, you can't be serious."

"I mean it all right. This time I really mean it."

She slammed down the receiver. At the other end, Terry could not quite take it all in.

After a good think, a few more drinks, and a nap, he decided the only course open to him was to have a good time in Sweden, and then face the music when he got back.

He met Maude. She was tall and suntanned, and the sweetest thing he'd ever seen. Maude wasn't worried about his career or where the next hit was coming from. She relaxed his troubled mind.

He was allowed to finish his two-week contract and after the show each night took her to dinner. She told him all about her family, who were well-to-do. Then one night they lingered too long at a dance. "It's too late for me to get home," she said pleadingly.

"Why not come to my hotel then? It's nice and cosy there." From the balcony they looked over the fairy lights in the trees of the big square below. He took her arm from around his, went inside and put Edna's photograph in his suitcase . . .

For the rest of his time in Sweden they were hardly apart. She was sad when he had to leave but smiled when he put her photograph in his wallet.

Terry headed straight for Edna's flat and walked in as if nothing had happened. But it had. Edna knew they were through.

She was firm. "We're finished," she said.

Terry accepted it surprisingly easily. He kissed her goodbye, packed his things and called a cab to take him back to mum and dad in their seventh-floor flat in Camberwell.

They tried to make a go of it again just once more while she was appearing in Ipswich.

"Let's go back together?" he pleaded.

"All right, Terry, we'll give it another try," sobbed Edna as she fell into his arms.

That night they stayed together. Terry was delighted; maybe they could make a go of it after all.

The next evening he was watching her in rehearsals, thinking and remembering. Remembering the times, those awful times when he had hung round while she worked. The times he was under a psychiatrist and Edna became the breadwinner.

That night, his old insecurity crept back. He lay in bed next to Edna, brooding. Then suddenly he said: "Edna, it's no good. I'm sorry, but it just won't work."

It was two o'clock in the morning.

*

That was the end of the marriage.

Edna told the *Daily Mirror*: "Terry Dene is NOT through, but I'm afraid our marriage IS."

There were only the formalities - the lawyer's letters, the evidence about Maude in Sweden, the divorce courts –to come.

*

Terry felt free at last. He didn't realise the skids were really under him. Now no one wanted to know him. He began to stay at home more and more and felt embarrassed to visit Soho in case he met someone he knew.

In the end he even felt scared to take his mum out in case she overheard some of the nasty cracks people hurled at him as he walked by.

The legal end for Edna and Terry came in the Divorce Court in June 1961, two years after the Swedish trip. It was on the ground of his "misconduct" with Maude.

Judge Glazebrook found that there was insufficient evidence against Maude, but found that Terry had committed misconduct.

Edna, too, admitted misconduct. The judge exercised discretion in respect of this and ordered Terry, then 22, to pay costs.

Later, at her tiny, pink-walled bed-sitter in George Street, Marylebone, Edna, still shaking and upset, talked to reporters.

"Now I must begin a new life. It's a fresh start for me completely. I have lots of plans for new records.

"After all, now my work is all I have to live for."

Looking tiny and rather helpless, she perched on her divan and said she was not bitter about the marriage. "Terry is a dear really, and has a wonderful sense of humour. I wish him well. If in the morning he came to the flat and told me he had no money and everything had gone wrong, I would give him my last ten shillings.

"You know, it was strange the last time we met - which was many months ago.

"We met over a coffee and we talked like two old friends, nothing more.

"I think he could be a great artist and I wish him the best of everything always."

In a soft voice she added: "Perhaps one day he'll meet the right girl."

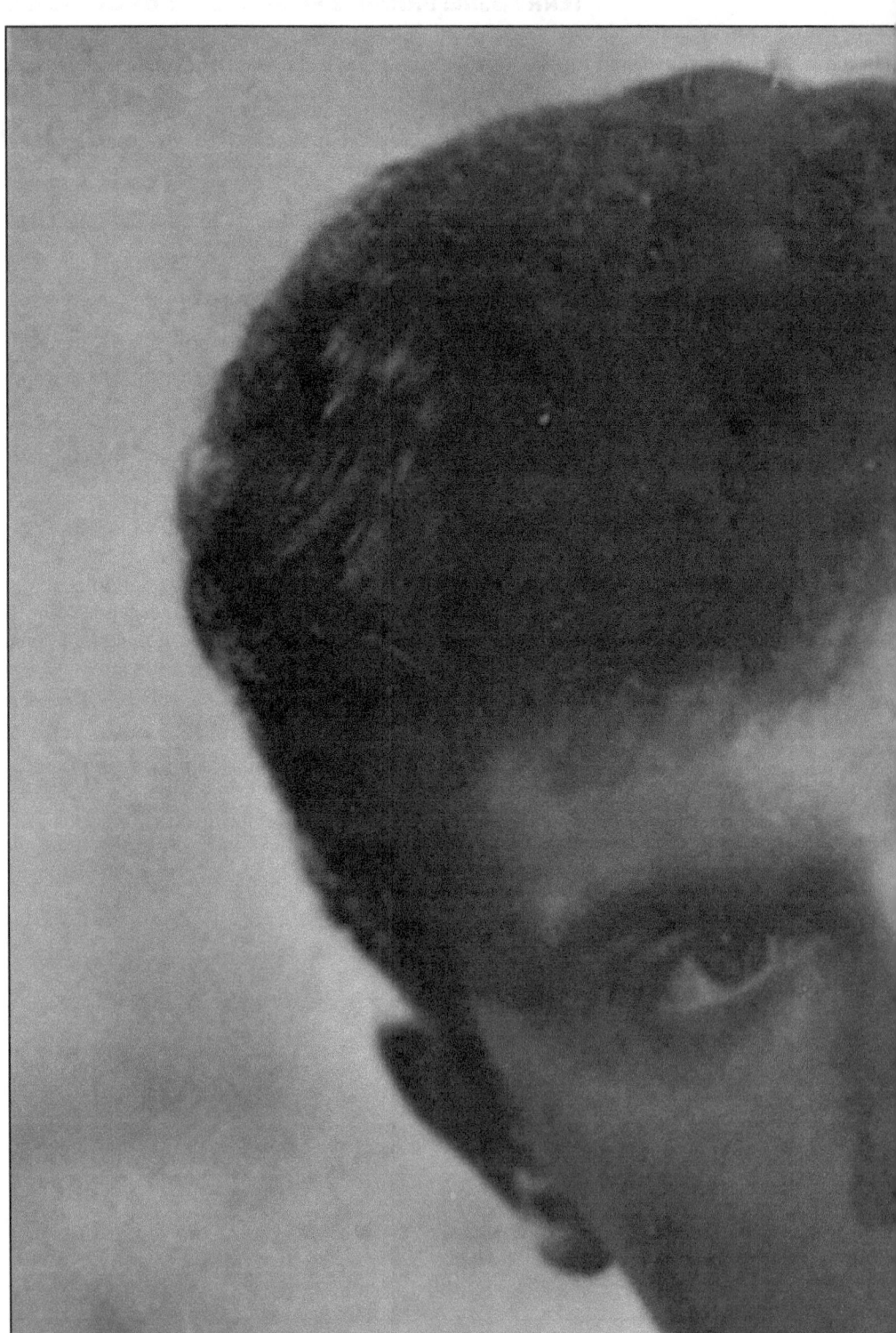

Chapter 19

The young frizzy-haired minister nervously approached the Southampton ballroom where Terry Dene was due to appear.

He adjusted his tie, brushed back his dark hair with his hand, cleared his throat, and then walked boldly into the foyer.

"Can I see Terry Dene, please?" he asked the manager. "I'm a Christian minister of religion and I'd like to talk to him."

"Hang on a minute, Vicar, and I'll see if he's free."

Terry's visitor was the Rev. Tony Stone, a Pentecostal minister who often visited show-biz personalities.

As the manager scurried away to search for the falling star, Tony fingered his black-bound pocket New Testament. It was afternoon and noisy rehearsals were in full swing.

It seemed like an eternity before Terry came over and asked, "Did you want to see me?"

"Yes, Terry," he said, extending his hand. "I'm a Christian minister. I realise that you are normally much too busy to come to see us, so I've come to you instead. It's become part of my ministry to visit stars to tell them about Jesus Christ."

Terry interrupted: "Well, you don't want to see me. I'm no star any more. I'm on the bottom rung of the ladder."

Tony's heart went out to the singer, as he went on: "Please pray for me. My life's in a terrible mess. My marriage finished, my career is nearly over because of the Army business, and I've just about had it with everything else."

Stone's heart melted at the meeting. For once, he was stumped for words. He had visited many other big names in show business - Tommy Steele, Craig Douglas, Cliff Richard - and had never before had any problem in communicating his faith. But somehow this was different. He was faced by a man who had apparently been totally crushed.

"I will pray for you," Tony promised as he left the ballroom. "I hope we meet again one day."

"I do hope so," said Terry, wearily returning to the back to go over a number. "Thanks for coming to see me. Not many people do that these days."

Tony Stone couldn't sleep that night. His thoughts kept going back to Terry. All he could do, as he tossed and turned in bed, was to pray out loud: "God, please help that boy. Please help him before it's too late."

*

In August 1963, Hymie Zahl died, forcing Terry to look for another manager. Soon he signed for Larry Parnes, a big-time manager who sold pop in bulk. All his boys were given fiery names - Fury, Wilde, Pride and Power, for example. Parnes was the model 50's manager. He was shrewd, quick-witted and had a natural flair for publicity. He made money and back-street kids into stars. But Dene was not one of his successes.

Terry was no longer a big name, and had to be content to tour the country with the other singers, near the bottom of the bill.

The Larry Parnes rock 'n' roll show included Terry's old drummer, Clem Cattini, in the backing group; later he was to work with the hit group *The Tornadoes*.

Terry would sit on his own in the coach, strumming his guitar in a corner and singing some of his numbers. The others would joke around or play cards. As the bus roared towards one date, Clem jokingly tossed a penny at Terry, saying: "Keep it for your troubles, Terry."

Terry went ashen. "I remember the day when you wouldn't have done that," he said.

Clem told me: "Terry was very sensitive and something like that hurt him deeply. Anybody else would have laughed it off, but Terry's reaction made me feel terrible."

During the Parnes tour, Terry again showed the infuriating side of his character. This time it was a case of Pride coming before a fall . . .

The running order for the first half of the hip-swinging show at the *Liverpool Empire* was Duffy Power, Terry Dene, Dickie Pride and then Billy Fury to top the half.

For three consecutive nights, Terry disappeared to a nearby pub for a few drinks as the show began. He hated being so low on the bill and sat tight until he knew he was too late for his spot and Pride had been forced to go on before him. Then he would reappear at the theatre, breathless and full of apologies.

"I didn't realise the time," he would mumble to anyone who would listen.

Meanwhile an angry Dickie Pride was seething because he had been forced down the bill by Terry's trick. He would go through his act and then storm off, muttering "I'll kill him, I'll kill him." Terry would keep out of his way, and then dash on and go through his act, a place higher on the bill.

But on the third night, Dickie came off shaking with anger and spotted Terry in the wings; he was late again. Pride stormed over and took an almighty swing at Terry's jaw knocking him out cold.

The other singers desperately tried to revive the unconscious Dene, while the M.C. held the fort with a string of corny jokes until Terry was in a fit state to do his spot.

Hal Carter, touring manager for the show, told me: "Terry never pulled that trick again. Dickie was a little chap with a quick temper, so naturally none of us provoked him in any way. But this business with Terry really upset him."

A dazed Dene struggled through his numbers and stumbled off stage, not quite knowing where he was. During the interval Billy Fury came into his dressing room and told Terry, "Dickie's in a right state over thumping you. He's been crying."

"I'm not too pleased myself," said Terry.

But he followed Fury into Pride's dressing-room and the pop pair shook hands.

"Sorry I hit you so hard, mate," said Dickie. "You deserved it, mind you, but I still went too far."

"That's all right, Dickie, I'm used to trouble. It's my middle name, didn't you know?"

It wasn't surprising that Terry didn't last long with the Parnes stable. He decided to keep trying, hoping against hope he'd be back on the top one day.

But the bubble had burst for Terry Dene. In 1961 he talked to a *Daily Mail* reporter as he sat in the Wardour Street, Soho club where he was booked to sing in the wee small hours of the morning to people beginning to wish they were in bed.

Gone were the screaming Dene-age fans with his name embroidered on their sweaters. The girls who once pushed him to the top in a hurry with their adoration were somewhere else. At somebody else's concerts. In someone else's fan club.

Terry sat there, a has-been at 22. In that short past, along with his broken career, was a broken marriage and a near broken mind.

He told the *Mail* man: "I don't have to kid you. You can see I'm not earning very much money any more. I've begun all over again. At the bottom. It's going to take a long time to get back to the top. Before, I went to the top quick, too quick.

TERRY DENE: BRITAIN'S FIRST ROCK AND ROLL REBEL

"Well, now I know there's no quick way to the top. They put a crown on your head and call you a star and give you a lot of money and you think 'Marvellous. I've made it big time!'

"You never think it can happen to you. Losing it all, I mean. You think it will last for ever, because you are young, I suppose. Seventeen I was when I started. Seventeen. You buy a lot of clothes, a car. You throw your money around and act crazy, like it's going to last for ever.

"Well, it don't. It don't last for ever. One day you wake up and it's over. No more bookings. No more £500 a week. No more fans. No nothing."

Dene, his face a white blob in the darkness, went on slowly, without emotion, "But I've no resentment. I now know you have to put something into life to get anything out of it, and I wasn't putting very much in, was I?

"At first, when I began slipping, I used to blame everybody and everything, but sooner or later you have to face reality. Well, I've reached that point now. I've learned to face reality."

Terry outlined his Army and marriage troubles, and added: "Maybe I can make a come-back. After all, I'm only 22. That's no age at all, really. 22. No age at all."

The reporter commented: "I hope Terry Dene makes it again. I really do. For few people can have suffered so much in the pursuit of success. Next time I think he will have learned its true value."

The only solace Terry had at this time was drink. He hit the bottle heavily, and once again was back in court. In November 1961, police arrested him in a Chelsea street at 3.10 a.m. and charged him with being drunk and disorderly and shouting.

At Marlborough Street Court, he asked for seven days to pay a 40p fine. "Things are pretty bad. I've got a lot of debts," he told the magistrate.

Then came another breakdown, this time during a £15 a night engagement at a Sheffield working men's club. Three hundred packed into the club to see Terry in action, but Terry decided he couldn't face them and returned to London.

Earlier he had been drinking in the club, and had signed scores of autographs for teenage fans. He laughed and joked with them, then left "to collect my music and guitar from my digs". He did - and caught the next train to London.

At the club there was some booing and foot stamping by teenage fans and many of them demanded their money back.

The Press were quickly on the story, and Terry's new manager, told the *Daily Mirro*: "He's at home with his mother in Camberwell, London – frightened, worried and completely exhausted. He felt so ill in Sheffield that he left without even seeing his landlady.

"He wants me to say to everyone up there that he's very sorry for his disappearance. Terry seems dogged by bad luck, but I think he'll still win through in the end."

The agent who booked Terry for the series of one-night stands in Yorkshire said: "He was on his way back to the top. He was going down big everywhere and the next week he should have appeared at the Festival Hall."

Davy Jones, later to star with top American group, The Monkees, took Terry's place for the remainder of the Yorkshire shows.

When he recovered from this breakdown, Terry went on stage again, but soon cracked. He couldn't face his audiences. In December 1961, when he should have sung at a comeback show in a Hertfordshire dance hall, he didn't even turn up and 300 angry teenagers were repaid their 17½p entrance money.

"I went down there but left because I could not face another audience," Terry explained afterwards. "I didn't feel too good. My arm was hurting. I decided I couldn't go on. I just went home to bed." Despondently he added, "I'd probably have been booed anyway."

Later, standing mournfully at the door of his parents' seventh-floor council flat in Camberwell, he said: "I'm giving up show business. A guy can only take so much."

It was teatime but Terry was dressed in pyjamas and a maroon dressing-gown. It was a week since his breakdown. He said he was going to look for an ordinary job. "I don't care what it is so long as it's far away from show business; I want to bury the name of Dene and forget all the past," he commented.

But the love-hate relationship with show business was to continue for some time yet.

Sometimes he would go along for the ride on dates with other artistes, and once he visited The Cavern, Liverpool, home of *The Beatles*, with Jimmy Justice and the *Ex-Checkers*. Raye Du-Val, colourful drummer with the *Ex-Checkers*, triple winner of the world non-stop drumming marathon contest, and founder of the Rock 'n' Roll Preservation Society, recalls the occasion: "Terry happened to be with us that night, and when it got around that he was in *The Cavern*, he was besieged by autograph hunters. In fact Jimmy lost a lot of glory that night."

Raye, by the way, regained his world drumming record in 1960 with a mind-boggling 100 hours 1 minute 42½ seconds, from a certain Rory Blackwell: they had long been rivals.

Terry decided to try again, this time touring with American singer Gene Pitney. Many of his fans turned up to cheer, hoping this time he would make it.

One of those fans was Gerald Petken of Dagenham, who told me: "The last I saw of Terry was in 1962 at the *Odeon Theatre*, Barking. He was dressed very smartly with blue velvet round his cuffs and collar, and looked very relaxed. He chose to sing ballads only, and I can remember the 'Birth of the Blues' going down very well indeed.

"He was, in fact, in very fine voice, and to my wife and I it looked as though he had made it at last, judging by the applause.

"But the Press gave his appearance very little coverage, considering it was a pretty big bill, and once again he faded into obscurity."

Terry tried another record, "Fever", on the Aral record label: but it made no impression on the record fans, and a very sick Terry Dene despaired. There seemed to be no cure for his fever.

Chapter 20

As the early sixties became the middle sixties, Terry Dene tasted the bitter fruits of failure. Bookings were drying up, and when he did get a date, he was booed more often than not. He got used to leaving the stage to the sound of taunts about his Army failure, his marriage, and his breakdowns. He had all the symptoms of a has-been, but now he combined them with the courage of an old-stager.

Terry's comebacks were becoming a joke and more and more people were turning their backs on him. But he found strange allies in the Kray twins, London's most notorious gangsters, now serving life sentences in Parkhurst Prison for murder.

Reggie and Ronnie met him in a club and invited him round to their fortress at Cedra Court, a luxury block of flats in Walthamstow, about five miles north of Vallance Road, their former Bethnal Green home. Soon Terry Dene was "in" and for six months he lived with the Krays.

[A copy of his recent record, "Call to the Wind", released by Pilgrim, was sent to the Krays in Parkhurst.]

"The twins knew Terry had suffered a lot with his nerves and they tried to get him to snap out of it," Mrs. Violet Kray, their mother, told me.

"He was really down on his luck and I think they felt sorry for him.

"My boys often helped people like Terry, but that never got publicity. The newspapers only printed the bad things."

Reggie Kray, in a letter from the maximum security block of Parkhurst, told me that Terry had a "quality about him that is hard to describe."

He added: "It was as if he had seen and done a lot for his age. He reminded me of Robert Ryan, the American actor, a man who was apparently sure of himself in a quiet way because he had done a lot of living."

But Terry had done a lot of dying too . . . in front of hostile audiences.

Then he met up with Rhet Stoller, a Jewish musician, and they worked together for a time. Rhet made Terry take religion seriously and for a time he even considered becoming a Jew. He knew he needed some kind of spiritual experience, but wasn't sure in what direction it lay.

At times he prayed desperately to God - whoever he was - for help. But his prayers, apparently, got no higher than the ceiling of his room.

He would stop musicians and ask, "Where can I find peace?" They would shake their heads, and say: "Don't ask me, man."

As the months went by, he became increasingly bitter about the music profession. He used to wander the streets of Soho, hoping against hope that someone would recognise him and give him work. He sat in sleazy clubs warning starry-eyed youngsters about the dangers of show business.

"Keep away from it," he told one boy clutching a guitar. "The music business could cost you your soul."

In July 1964, he told the *Daily Mail*: "Since Christmas I have been trying to find a job, but every time they find out who I am they say no.

"People say they would like to help but 'can't think of anything at the moment'. So I stick around just waiting.

"I am living with my mum and dad in the flat now. I have just heard they're looking for assistants in a guitar shop in the West End. I may try for that . . ."

But, of course, he didn't.

He was now at his wits' end. Was there no one who could help him?

Then one night in bed he had a strange vision. As he lay restlessly in his darkened room he saw, in a dream, Christ on the cross. There were nails through His hands and His face was contorted in agony. It seemed He was sacrificing Himself for Terry's sins. As Terry dreamed, the crucified Christ fell towards him and crashed onto his shoulder.

"It was as if Jesus was saying, 'You don't have to suffer any more for your sins, I've taken them away on the cross'," Terry told me later.

"I was trembling when I woke up. I didn't know what to do. It was a wonderful, yet terrifying feeling. For a long time I had been punishing myself for my past, and here was Christ telling me to stop it."

With perspiration pouring off his forehead, Terry prayed fervently: "God, if you don't do something soon, I don't know what I'll do."

But God did.

It was a bright day in September 1964, but Terry was feeling far from bright as he wandered alone around the West End.

"There's Terry Dene," said a teenage girl on the arm of her boyfriend. "He was good - once."

He made his way towards Trafalgar Square and, as he passed by St. Martin's-in-the-Fields Church, a group of Christians came into view. They were handing out leaflets near a white mini-van which had a banner reading "JESUS CHRIST - THE SAME YESTERDAY, TODAY AND FOREVER" draped across the roof.

A smiling man handed him a tract, and Terry took it.

After scanning it, Terry said: "I believe in God. Where is He?"

"How much time can you spare?" said Ron Mulcah, a member of the group - the *Mobile Evangelistic Crusade.*

"I've got all the time in the world."

Ron guided Terry into the van and they were soon deep in conversation. As they talked, Terry felt a warmth inside which he had never experienced before. He told Mulcah of his past, of his much-publicised troubles.

It was only then that Ron realised he was talking to Terry Dene. He looked so different from his Press pictures. He had iron-grey hair, and his face looked pale and lined with pain.

"Look," said Terry, "I've been rich and successful, but it's never given me peace or happiness. I've come to my wits' end. I need help, and badly."

Ron began to tell Terry of the experiences which had led up to his own commitment to Christ. Terry sat spellbound, as the traffic roared by, and drank in every word. Here was someone who apparently didn't want to use him for gain or insult him, but was giving him something for free.

"Look, I've prayed many times, but nothing's happened."

"What do you mean, nothing's happened? Today's happened. You've been brought here for a purpose. Do you realise, Terry that Jesus has died for our sins, yours and mine? He can forgive. Why don't you accept Him into your life? Things will be different if you do."

"All right, what can I lose? What do I have to do?"

Mulcah asked him just to pray with him, repeating the words. He told Terry to confess he was a sinner and to ask Christ to forgive his sins and come into his life.

Terry stumbled over the words, but still they came out. Suddenly he felt lighter, cleaner. His face was flushed, and he felt a new lightness.

"We would like to keep in touch with you, Terry," said Ron Howe, a gaunt-looking man who led the evangelistic group, as he was introduced to the pop singer outside the van.

"Sure," said Terry. "I'll give you my address."

With that, Terry bounced from the van, caught the bus back to his parents' high-rise Camberwell flat and told them the whole story of his "conversion".

That night he went out to celebrate. He walked into his regular drinking club, a huge smile on his face. It was a hang-out for show business people looking for work.

"What's the matter, Terry? Won the pools?" asked a drinking pal.

"No, mate, I've just become a Christian."

And Terry Dene got pleasantly tiddly.

*

It looked as though his life had taken a turn for the better. To cap everything, his agent got him his first job for months, a short run at a Blackpool night spot.

But soon Terry got up to his old tricks. He was regularly late appearing, and there was no enthusiasm when he went through his tired routine. He felt it was farcical singing love songs to mythical girls.

His drinking began all over again, and doubts about what he had done in London tormented him. "Have I become a new person, like the man said, or is it just a confidence trick?" kept asking himself.

One night he met a shapely girl on the Golden Mile and decided to ask her back to his hotel room for some fun. She proudly held his arm as they threaded their way through the crowds and past a parade of shops. Then Terry stopped to look in a bookshop window. The only thing he could see was a huge black Bible for sale, and something inside him told him to go in and buy it.

"Wait a minute," he said. "I'm just going to buy that Bible."

The girl was staggered as Terry disappeared into the shop, to re-emerge minutes later with a King James Version Bible. He winked at the girl, allowing her to clasp one arm and proudly tucking the Bible under the other. He spent that night tucked up not with the girl, but the Bible.

Terry spent every spare moment that week ploughing through the first five books of the Old Testament.

"I didn't understand much of what I was reading," he said. "But I knew it was God's word, so I felt I just had to read it."

Each night after the show, he would head for his bedroom and read into the early hours. He longed to talk to someone about God, but didn't know anyone in Blackpool to turn to. Something very strange was happening to him, but he couldn't understand what it was.

"I realise now it was God at work," he told me. "At that time I didn't understand these things."

His stage performances were going from bad to worse, and one night the irate club owner decided to confront him. "If you don't pull your socks up, lad, you're out," he said in a broad Lancashire accent. "I mean it, lad. You'll be out."

"There's no need to sack me," said Terry. "I quit. I've had enough of this lousy business."

"No need to be like that, lad. I was only warning you."

"Warning or not, I've given my last show."

And he meant it. It was the last time he appeared anywhere professionally. At last Terry Dene had left the business which had scarred him so badly.

*

Terry caught the first train back to London, and headed over to see George Cooper, his agent. He told him to cancel all future engagements.

"It's the end of my career, George," he told him. "My future's in God's hands now."

Terry had realised that the only way he could get real peace of mind was by total commitment to Christianity. There could be no compromise.

During this period, Ron Howe and his colleagues had paid several visits to Terry's home, only to be told by his mother that Terry was away. They had almost despaired of seeing him again.

But now it was Terry's turn to search the streets of Soho, trying to catch a glimpse of the white mini-van. He was bursting to tell the two Rons his news, and to pose scores of questions about what he had been reading in the Bible.

Finally, after several frustrating days, he found the van parked off the Strand. Terry ran towards it and was greeted with a huge smile from Ron Howe and handshakes all round from the rest of the group.

He was near to tears. He was back among friends.

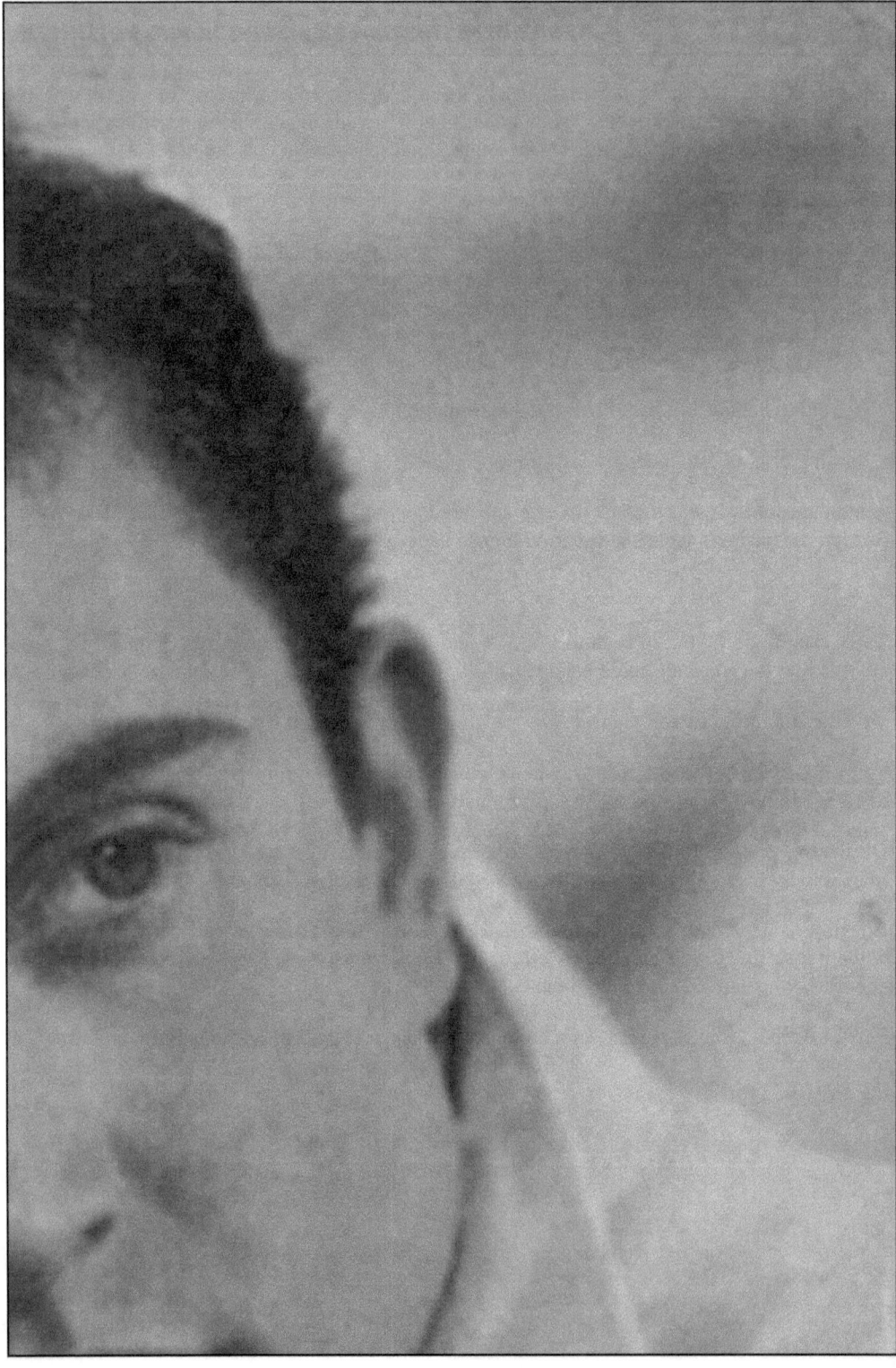

Chapter 21

It was late evening when the phone rang at Joan Howe's Barnet home. Wearily she picked up the receiver.

"Hello, Joan. It's Ron here. Look, we've come across this Terry Dene chap again - you know, the ex-pop star. I told you he had decided to become a Christian, didn't I? Is it all right to bring him over tonight? He would like to stay for a few days."

"All right, bring him back. I'll get the supper on." Ron's wife was now used to unusual visitors to her five-bedroomed house. Howe was constantly contacting people during his evangelistic forays into London and bringing them home. Some were strange, to say the least. One bit Joan in the arm during a fit of temper, another dug up the lawn "for something to do".

When Terry arrived, Joan greeted him warmly. "So you're Terry Dene," she said brightly, taking his coat.

"No, Mrs. Howe. My name is Terry Williams. Terry Dene no longer exists."

Joan was rather taken aback, but asked her guest to make himself feel at home. His iron-grey hair made him quite handsome, she thought.

Ron took Terry to see his room, introduced him to their three children, and after a light supper, they had a short time of prayer and a Bible reading.

As Terry snuggled under the covers that night, he was a happy man. Peace was not a faraway dream any more, it was becoming a reality.

Daily, Ron and Joan took the eager Terry through the Scriptures, helping him to grow as a Christian. Soon he joined the team for evangelistic trips into Soho.

In the light of tawdry neon strip-club signs, Terry Williams told inquisitive crowds of his downfall and how God rescued him. They listened respectfully. There were no longer any cat-calls.

Word soon spread about Terry's conversion, with the result that one day he was picked up by the Barnet police. The cops had heard the former rock-star was living on their patch, so they called round to ask him to "accompany us to the station".

Once there, they fired questions at Terry about the Mobile Evangelistic Crusade, and, when they were satisfied there was nothing criminal going on, they let him go. Ron collected him from the station.

*

The group was Pentecostal and many of the gifts of the Spirit were being used. One evening Terry attended a meeting where prayers were offered for healing.

"I had suffered from nervous trouble since I was three years old, and so I decided to go forward," said Terry. "During the prayers I found myself crying and all my depression lifted from me. I felt completely healed."

He also received the "baptism of the Holy Spirit" and, after hands had been laid on him, spoke with other tongues. He was then baptised in water at a Brixton Baptist church.

Everything was so new and exciting for such a deprived person. He was experiencing happiness he never knew existed.

Soon the Press picked up the news of his conversion and swooped. Splash stories, mostly sympathetic, appeared in many of the nationals about "The New Terry Dene – Sorry Williams".

Len Adams wrote in *The People*: "One-time rock 'n' roll star Terry Dene, whose sensational career as a pop singer crumbled in ruins after a nervous breakdown, has seen the light.

"He has stopped smoking and drinking, renounced all worldly goods, and is working as a full-time unpaid evangelist, handing out religious tracts and preaching the Gospel on the street corners of Soho."

Terry told Adams: "Later, when I'm fully trained, I hope to become a minister. My future is with the Lord.

"I am happier here than I have ever been. It is like being born all over again."

At every opportunity, Terry was telling crowds and individuals about his new life in Christ. One day he was speaking at an open-air meeting in Victoria Park, Finchley, when another young man who had recently surrendered his life to Christ, joined the crowd - Cliff Richard.

"I had heard about his stand and I wanted to hear what he had to say," Cliff told me. "I was very impressed and encouraged by his testimony.

"He had changed completely from when I last saw him. His hair was white, but he seemed to have matured as a person. He obviously no longer had the nervous problems which had so beset his career.

"I stood at the back of the crowd and wore my glasses, hoping people wouldn't recognise me. I expect that to this day, Terry doesn't know I was in the crowd."

A few years later Terry and Cliff met over a meal in London and were able to discuss how the Lord had guided them - in different directions. Each respects what the other is doing.

As Terry slowly grew in faith, Ron, who worked as a free-lance photographer, suggested he should get a job. So Terry started work at a market-garden about five miles from the Howe's home, picking cucumbers in hothouses. He oiled his old bike and cycled over there each day; but he soon found he hated the job, working hour after hour in the sweltering heat. He was exhausted when he came in.

Some nights he went up to bed to lie down and recover. One evening Joan heard strange sounds coming from his room, and went up to investigate.

When she opened the door, Terry jumped up, blinked his glazed eyes, and told her he had had an hallucination. "Hundreds of cucumbers were falling down round me." he said. "It was terrible. I thought I'd be buried by them."

Not surprisingly, that job didn't last long.

*

At the Howes, Terry would entertain Joan's 86-year-old mother, Ada, with his music. He sat for hours at the piano and played while she sat back and enjoyed it. Music was of great therapeutic value to Terry at this time -as it still is.

Different full-time jobs were found for Terry during his nine-month stay with the Howes; he worked as a chauffeur-gardener for a business man and also as a packer with Scripture Union in London, but he found it hard to stick at any of them for very long.

Ron Howe died at Christmas 1972. Before his death he wrote to me: "The very thought of discipline and work would make Terry ill, yet he was not lazy in the ordinary sense. He wanted to be able to work, but it seemed his undisciplined childhood and the easy way money came to him as a star had conditioned his mind to this way of life."

Terry tried hard to fit into the orthodox work pattern, but he never succeeded. It was a foreign concept to him. Before he had toured the country, working irregular hours. Now all he wanted to do was to serve the Lord and study the Bible.

Ron would give him odd jobs to keep him occupied and Terry would set to. He was slow, but always did a good job. Joan remembers it well. "If you would ask him to wash up the dishes he would take hours, but when he had finished, everything was gleaming."

Once he was asked to repair a fence at the rear of Ron's mother's home. He took nearly a week to do it, but did it well. All the time he worked, Terry sang his head off. Who could blame him? Now he had something to sing about.

Chapter 22

Terry Dene the hell-raising pop star was gone, and so was his talent. For Terry Williams had decided he no longer wanted anything to do with his painful past. He discarded his guitar, his records, and his show-biz name, and set about a serious study of the Scriptures. He witnessed in the West End and occasionally spoke at meetings, but vowed never again to strum a guitar, swivel a hip or even sing in public.

He didn't want any links with Terry Dene. None of the members of the Mobile Evangelistic Crusade was allowed to call him Dene; it was Terry Williams, a plain ordinary guy, from now on.

But after several months without music Terry began to get restless. It was like having an arm amputated, and he began to pine. He knew he had talent and wasn't using it for God - but should he?

"I didn't want to start again just because I felt like it," he told me. "I wanted a definite sign from the Lord.

"So I prayed and asked the Lord to give me a guitar as a sign that He wanted me to start again."

It wasn't long before Terry got his "sign". The Crusade was having a week away from it all at Folkestone, when the heaven-sent guitar came his way. The party spent the time witnessing on the beach, studying the Bible together, and praying.

For Terry, it was sheer heaven. These were people he loved and trusted. He relaxed with them. They weren't interested in 10% cuts and the fine print on contracts, they just welcomed him as a brother. And "Brother" Terry began to grow as a person. He had been deprived of much of the best in life for so long, and he now had a lot to make up.

He was deep in thought as he strolled through the hotel lobby and was stopped by the manager, who was clutching a guitar. "Terry, I hope you won't be offended, but I have this guitar, and I can't play a note. It seems such a waste. I feel the Lord wants you to have it."

Terry's heart leapt with excitement. Could this be the sign he wanted? He missed his music, but still wasn't convinced his prayer had been answered.

"Ron," he said, stopping his friend and leader. "I've been offered a guitar by the hotel manager.

"I asked the Lord to give me a sign that I should start singing again, and it looks like He has. Should I take it?"

"Why are you waiting?" replied Ron Howe. "I want to be the first to witness your comeback for the Lord!"

A beaming smile covered Terry's pale face as he bounded off to collect the instrument. It wasn't up to the professional standard he was used to, but he wasn't complaining - it was a guitar.

He took it off to a corner of the lounge and began strumming. He fondled it lovingly, then sang a few uncertain notes. Time stood still for a moment, and the chattering ceased as Terry's voice falteringly, then confidently burst into song again, and his fingers found the chords on the guitar. His eyes lit up, his face shone, as he sang. It was an apt choice. "I Believe in Miracles." He was like a child with a new toy and wouldn't be parted from the guitar for the rest of the week.

"Because of my life, I saw many things as evil. One of those things was the guitar, but I soon realised that it wasn't the instrument that was evil, but the way it was used," Terry said.

Soon Terry was singing at meetings and allowed himself, after pressure from Ron Howe, to be billed as Terry Dene, former rock 'n' roll idol who found Christ.

Terry Dene was also the name on the tract he wrote about his conversion.

"Today I am far from the bright lights and the glamour, but I am truly happier than I have ever been," he declared. "Many young people desire fame, prestige, clothes, money. But none of these satisfy. I know. I've had them all in abundance, and from my own hard experience I can honestly say that nothing - nothing at all -can compare with the joy of knowing Jesus and being at peace with God."

After about nine months with the Howes, Terry was straining at the leash. He had learned many important lessons about the Christian faith, and was longing to move further afield. Being used to travelling, he found it burdensome being stuck in one place.

So when Ron suggested he might like to move to Bristol and work with evangelist Peter Newman, he jumped at the idea.

The burly Newman had met Terry during a visit to the Howes, and was not sure whether he could take the one-time idol on. But finally he agreed and Terry duly arrived full of enthusiasm at his house.

Peter Newman, a tough character who once had a serious drinking problem himself had experienced a life-changing conversion, and was dedicating himself to helping problem people.

He taught Terry many lessons as they travelled round the country together, Peter preaching and Terry singing and giving his testimony.

Often Terry's moods would swing like a pendulum. His love for God was real, and he wanted to be a better Christian, so when these black moods came he felt anguished because he thought he was letting the Lord down.

His guilt complexes caused many problems. At times he couldn't face congregations because he felt so unworthy. He confided in Peter that because of his past life he felt he couldn't glorify his Lord.

Peter told me: "One could never be sure of him or what his spiritual temperature was going to be at a crusade or meeting. If it was low, it meant me spending a lot of time with him and his problems; if he was spiritually on top, I would have to watch him, afraid to leave him alone, especially with people we were staying with, because he would often exhort them and rebuke them with very little wisdom."

Peter Newman, who, at the time directed the New Man Trust, a recognised Home Office hostel in Liskeard, Cornwall, feels that many of Terry's early problems as a Christian stemmed from others using him for propaganda.

"He was never allowed to forget he was Terry Dene," Newman said. "At times I believe he revelled in it, and at other times it disgusted him and he would say 'If I had never been Terry Dene, they wouldn't want me.'

"I often tried to get him to drop the big name image, and he would agree, but when it came to the actual moment, he would hold back. I wasn't concerned about his value as a witness to Christ because he was once Terry Dene: I wanted Terry Williams to have a deep faith in God 24 hours a day, and that's what he wanted for himself. But he was forever in the limelight."

He added: "Despite all I have said, Terry was one of the most honest and sincere Christians that I have ever known. To say that God never blessed his efforts would be untrue, because many a time God's blessing was upon his singing and testimony.

"Others only saw Terry 'switched on', but those of us who lived with him knew what a battle he had to endure. I loved him as a true brother and my family loved him too."

So Terry's problems were not gone completely because of his decision to follow Christ. Edna told me: "I believe Terry still has the same problems to face as he did when we were married, but now he has help with them. I can't say any more than that."

That was the key to Terry's new life. He had help, spiritual help. He had friends to turn to, and instead of hitting the bottle, he talked to them. But besides these friends, he talked to the Lord. Terry spent many hours confiding his innermost fears in prayer and he also learned to praise in prayer.

TERRY DENE: BRITAIN'S FIRST ROCK AND ROLL REBEL

During Terry's time with Peter Newman, he sang in a church in South Wales, and a local minister who had heard of his visit decided to make the journey to see him.

The Rev. Tony Stone handed his visiting card to a church member, and asked if it could be taken to Terry in the vestry. Within seconds a puzzled singer emerged and looked at the minister. "Do you want me?" he asked. There was something vaguely familiar about the man, but he just couldn't place where he had seen him before.

"Do you remember me, Terry? When you were still in the business, I came to see you at a Southampton ballroom. I read of your conversion and I wanted to see you again, mainly to tell you I have prayed for you ever since we met. I felt if anyone needed God, you did."

"Thanks! Do you know I've had letters from believers all over the country saying they too had been praying for me. It's great their prayers have been answered."

Tony Stone noted the difference in the singer since their last meeting. He was much more at ease and no longer looked as if his world was about to cave in on him.

Shortly afterwards, Tony invited Terry to his church to take part in meetings, and they soon struck up a deep friendship which finally resulted in Tony Stone becoming Terry's adviser and handling all his affairs.

During Terry's visit to Tony's church, a message came from the local cottage hospital that a 13-year-old boy from the church had been admitted for minor surgery. They thought it would be nice if Terry went into the ward and sang for the youngster and other patients.

The hospital authorities gave the go-ahead, and in strode Terry with his guitar. A grey-haired, pyjama-clad patient gasped as he saw him.

"Terry Dene! TERRY DENE: Britain's first Rock and Roll Rebel," he said loudly.

Terry stopped and said: "That's right; the old Terry Dene is dead. You're looking at the new one!"

Peter Newman and Terry finally parted company and he teamed up with a West Indian preacher called Ken McCarthy. Working with Ken was an enjoyable experience for Terry, for he greatly enjoyed the freedom of worship in West Indian meetings. Choruses were sung over and over again, and hands were pumped in time with the beat. Preachers were joyfully supported from the floor with cries of "Amen" and "Praise the Lord". Terry learned to shout them as loud as the rest. He felt an affinity with his black-skinned brothers and sisters, but wasn't sure how to take one remark after a particularly lively meeting.

"Terry," a man said, clasping his hand around his shoulder, "You're the only white man I know with a black heart!"

Terry spent about 18 months with Ken McCarthy and travelled thousands of miles around Britain and Europe singing, testifying and also being grounded in the Scriptures by the evangelist.

To Terry's great delight, he also worked with a West Indian group modelled on *The Shadows*, called the *Soul Seekers*, and even cut an EP with them on the Herald label. The songs included "One Day, Down from His Glory" (to the tune of "O Sole Mio") and "Just Call on the Name of Jesus".

Terry also made a series of straight from the shoulder evangelistic programmes for the pirate radio show, Radio Caroline, with McCarthy and the Soul Seekers. The programme was called Impact, and brought in a steady mail from interested listeners.

A trip to Sweden with Ken McCarthy was another attractive prospect. Ken had booked meetings in Gothenburg and took Terry along to sing.

As Terry walked down the gang-plank from the ferry at the Swedish port, he never guessed that his life was soon to take an unexpected turn. But turn it did.

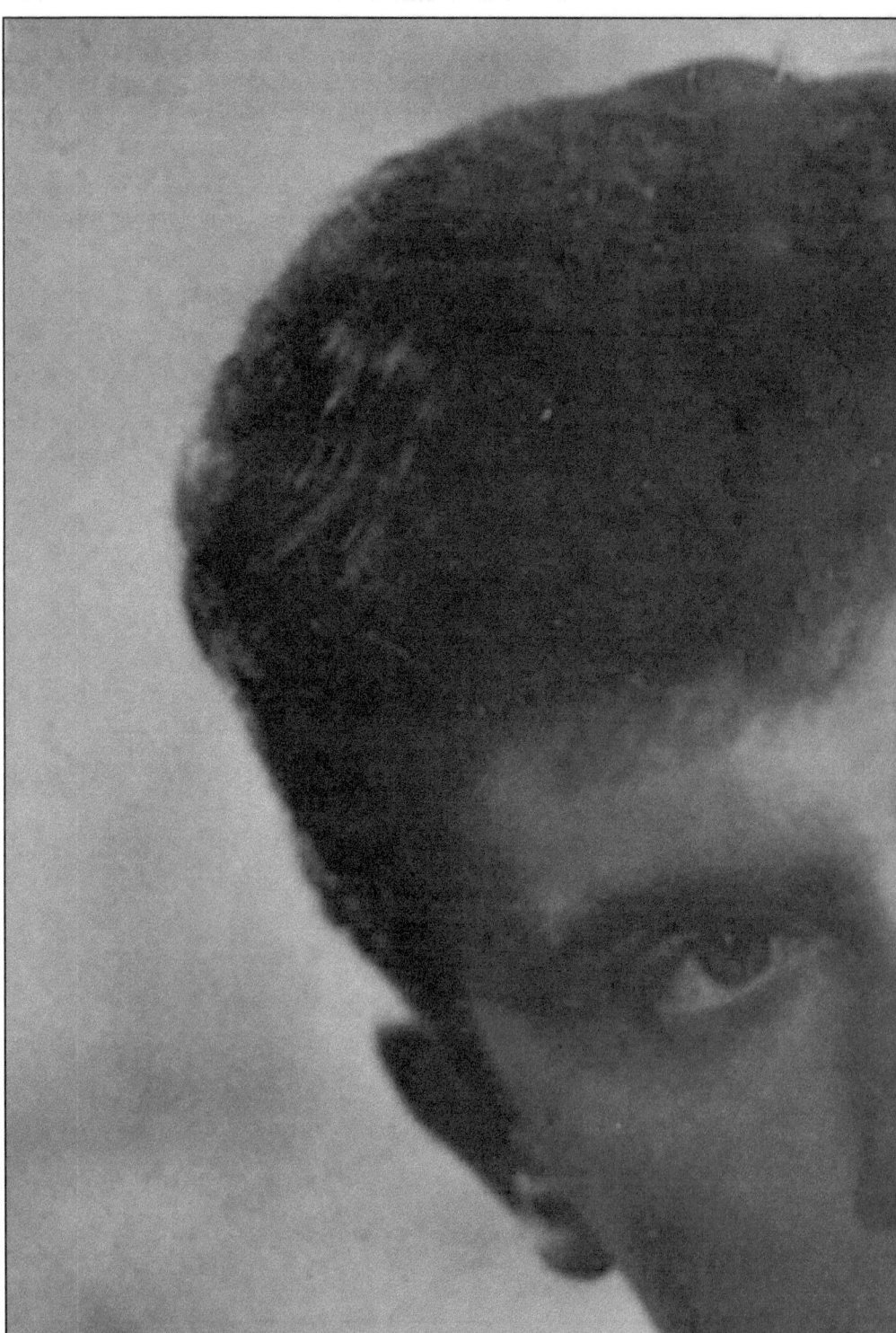

Chapter 23

Margaretta, a pretty dark-haired nurse, had been an Elvis fan for many years. She had carried his name emblazoned on her duffle bags, listened to his records and watched all his films.

But she had never heard of his British counterpart, Terry Dene. So when she saw in a Gothenburg newspaper that an English singer of that name was singing at a local church, the prospect did not exactly have her leaping for joy. It did, however, provoke enough interest for her to give up a free afternoon to walk to the church and settle in at the back to listen to him.

With the help of an interpreter, Terry introduced himself, and began singing with the guitar. He looked older than the nurse had expected. His white hair disguised his real age, and the blue lines of suffering under his eyes added 20 years to him. But when he sang, his whole face shone, his eyes most of all.

Margaretta felt a strange attraction to him. The feeling was two-way because all through the meeting, and through Ken McCarthy's fiery sermon, Terry's eyes were fixed on hers. She gazed back.

Margaretta didn't realise at the time, but she was in an old people's meeting.

"She was the nicest old-age pensioner I had ever seen," Terry joked later.

He feared she would dash out at the end of the meeting - realising her mistake - so he was over the moon when she came up to him and spoke in clear English. "Thank you very much for your singing. I really enjoyed it," she said.

"That's very kind of you. God bless you," he replied.

Terry was used to young ladies at churches being friendly, for, despite his older looks, he still had the charm which wowed the girls.

But this girl was different somehow, and he felt his face flush as he tried to keep up the small-talk.

"I'm here again tonight, if you can make it," was his parting remark as she disappeared through the door.

"I'll try and get along," she turned and said. Margaretta was staying with an aunt and told her of the English singer she had seen. "I might go back tonight," she said.

But she was not there for the evening meeting, and Terry was deeply upset as he scanned the sea of faces. Used to disappointments, he engrossed himself in the community hymn singing, until he felt his eyes drawn to the back of the hall and saw Margaretta drifting in and being directed to a seat. She sat, bowed her head, whispered a quick prayer, and then stood with the rest of the people. As she began singing, she smiled at Terry. He went weak at the knees.

He was hooked - well hooked. Terry felt an excitement in his heart he had not known for many years. He had been out with lots of girls since Edna, but none affected him like this fresh-faced Swedish nurse.

They chatted like a couple of school kids after the meeting, and in between the polite handshakes Terry was dishing out to the congregation, Margaretta promised to return again if her duty roster allowed.

At the third meeting, Terry plucked up courage to ask for her name and address. "Ken and myself are off for another meeting in Sweden and then we're going to Austria. I would like to write to you if I could," he said hopefully.

Margaretta obliged. They shook hands and the couple went their separate ways, wondering if they really would ever meet again.

"I couldn't sleep thinking about him," Margaretta told me. "He phoned me several times before leaving Sweden."

Every other moment, Terry's thoughts kept returning to the girl who had affected him so deeply.

Maybe . . . maybe they could get married.

No, that was a silly thought. After all, he had made a disaster of his last marriage attempt.

In Austria, during a moment of impulse, he picked up the telephone and asked for a collect charge call to Sweden. He hadn't enough money to pay for the call, so got Margaretta to cover the cost. He timed the call well, for she was in and was delighted to hear from him. "I think we ought to get to know each other much better," bubbled Terry, thrilled he hadn't been rebuffed.

"I think that's a good plan," she replied. "Why not come and spend Christmas with my family and myself?"

"What a great idea!" Terry was overwhelmed. "Look, I'm going to England soon. I'll write from there: I'd better not phone again because I've cost you enough already."

Terry was restless when he returned home with the West Indian preacher. He found it hard to read his Bible and pray, for his concentration was focused on Margaretta. He read in the Old Testament about Gideon putting out a fleece to God, and decided to do the same himself. He prayed that if the Lord wanted them to link lives, He would get her parents to accept him.

The ex-pop star was extremely conscious of his previous life and was frightened that Margaretta's parents - a former Swedish policeman and his wife, both committed Christians - would not approve of a tearaway in the family.

Christmas 1968 with her family was to be the test. Although they hardly knew each other, the love-bug was hard at work and Terry again set sail for Gothenburg.

Margaretta met him at the docks and they headed for the Christmas holiday retreat, a house on an island.

"Do you think your parents will like me?" Terry kept asking, full of doubts.

"Don't worry," she reassured him. "If the Lord is in this, they will like you."

They liked him. The singing evangelist was welcomed and immediately felt at home with them. He couldn't speak their language and they didn't know his, but their common faith forged an immediate link.

Margaretta sat between them and had great difficulty keeping up with the interpreting she was required to do. Words just bubbled from Terry, and although Margaretta missed some of them, her parents sat and nodded and smiled. They liked the look of this Englishman."

In their moments together, the lovers talked and talked. Terry told Margaretta snippets about his past – a little at a time, in case she was too shocked. She wasn't, because she realised they took place before Terry became a Christian.

They decided the "fleece" had been answered, and began seriously to plan the wedding date. It was to be in Margaretta's home town of Sveg, in central Sweden, a town of 2,500 souls where her father had been a policeman for many years.

The imposing Lutheran church dominates the town, and on March 22nd, 1969, the couple met in the entrance to follow the Swedish custom of bride and groom walking down the aisle together.

Terry felt terrible! It was far worse than he had felt before shows. For if he fluffed this one, his life would be hell. In the entrance, carved in Swedish in the stone, he noticed the words "God bless your going in and your going out, from now and for ever more".

As they linked arms and began walking up the aisle, Margaretta sneaked a look at her husband-to-be. "He was as white as a sheet and looked straight ahead," she recalls. "I don't think I have ever seen anyone look so white."

Somehow Terry mouthed his vows. Margaretta said them firmly, without nerves.

I walked down that aisle with Terry when I visited him in Sweden to research this book. He told me he would like to go through the ceremony again because he feels that now he would understand the vows he took. He was in such a state of nerves at the time that very little penetrated.

"It was so different from when I married Edna," he said as we stood at the altar rails. "That was like a contract you signed to do a week of shows. That's all it was. This one was for real."

The 117 guests packed into a hall across the road, tucked into a meal and then listened to the speeches. The highlight of the proceedings came when Terry and Margaretta sang a duet with the words "Alleu, Alleu, Allelujah, Praise the Lord". They looked into each other's eyes and smiled, for they had good reason to praise the Lord.

They spent their first night in a Sveg flat: no calls to psychiatrists, no Press men on hand to record every word, no crowds of sensation-seekers lighting for a glance of Terry. It was just a couple from a couple of countries, deeply in love, and happy to share the rest of their lives.

After a week in Sveg, they loaded up a car and drove to Gothenburg and, after a short ferry trip, crossed Germany, Holland and Belgium to catch the boat to Britain at Ostend.

They stayed with Terry's parents and visited many of his relatives and friends, including Ron Howe in Barnet. Terry re-lived his life to his wife as they drove around London, and Margaretta soon realised her husband was something of a controversial character in his home land.

"I don't think I would have liked to know the old Terry Dene," she told me.

The couple agreed that their new home would be in Krlbo in Sweden and Terry would start to take bookings as a free-lance travelling evangelist, while Margaretta would work in a local hospital to boost the poor money which his outreach work would bring in.

Soon Terry realised that life in Sweden wasn't going to be as easy as he had first hoped. He was an outsider, he spoke only a few words of the difficult language, and he didn't understand the ways of these silent, unemotional people.

"When I first came to Sweden with Ken McCarthy, it was great. We had an interpreter and it was like a great holiday," said Terry. "But you can get misconceptions from holidays. I found it very difficult to get down to learning the language and understanding the ways of Sweden."

The couple would talk in Swedish whenever possible but Margaretta would give Terry a rest when she saw he was having trouble.

"He would come back from meetings tired and exhausted, so I would talk to him in English," she said. "People told me I was wrong and should have talked in Swedish all the time, but I disagreed."

Slowly, very slowly, Terry got the hang of the language, and like a child began to string words together. Always a good mimic, he began to speak passable Swedish, with the local accent.

Being away from Britain did much to heal the scars of his past. People in Sweden didn't know much about Terry, and so he was not an outcast.

Expressen, the country's top paper, carried a feature on Terry: "Do you remember rock 'n' roll idol Terry Dene?" It did nothing but good, because bookings from churches around the land flooded in, meaning that Terry was kept busy. He was away for weeks at a time, singing, preaching, and talking directly to people. He cut an LP, partly in Swedish and partly in English.

The rock 'n' roll singer was now singing a new tune - to the Lord.

Chapter 24

"Fasten your seat-belts, ladies and gentlemen. We are about to land at Stockholm Airport."

As I hastily fastened my seat belt into place I wondered what my stay with Terry and Margaretta would be like. I had met them briefly in London to agree plans for my visits. Most of the research was done; now I was to meet them and see what they were really like.

Surely Terry could never have done the things he was supposed to have done? Was he really now a committed Christian, or was it just another gimmick in his life?

Margaretta waved as I emerged with my suitcase from customs. "Had a good trip?" she asked brightly. "Sorry Terry couldn't make it, but he's finishing a week's crusade and should be back tonight."

As I clambered into the couple's red Saab, I noticed a text in Swedish stuck on the rear window. Margaretta translated: "It says: 'Believe in the Lord Jesus Christ and you shall be saved'."

The engine roared into life and Margaretta put me at ease with a smile. At first neither of us knew what to say, but soon we relaxed and Margaretta told me she was taking me to a friend in Stockholm. "She's going to give us breakfast and you can have a lie down," she told me.

Pine trees flashed by as Mrs. Terry Williams talked about life with her one-time hell-raising husband. "He's told me all about his past, you know. Terry still does silly things. Do you know he once came to meet me at the hospital dressed in an old overcoat and hat. At first I didn't recognise him. When I asked him what he was playing at, he said he had felt sorry for a friend because of the cold weather and so swopped his new overcoat for the man's old coat and hat.

"I couldn't really scold him because his heart was in the right place."

I warmed to Margaretta as she chattered away about her impressions of England from her last trip. "I didn't realise there were so many slums . . . it seemed very dirty compared with Sweden."

As we reached Stockholm, she asked: "Like to see around before we go to my friends?"

I nodded. It was only about 8 a.m. and I was anxious to see as much as possible of Sweden, fearing I would be cooped up in Terry's flat for the rest of the week, frantically note-taking.

We cruised around the spotless city with Margaretta pointing out the main landmarks, obviously very proud of her capital. She parked the car and we wandered around the city as it awoke from sleep. She took me for a ride on the city's underground. Then we had a bite of breakfast at the main railway station café.

After a short rest at her friend's home it was time to set off for other friends in the university town of Upsala. I asked Margaretta why all the motorists had their headlights switched on although it was daylight. "We always do that," she replied. "It is so people can see us better."

The tea at Upsala was entertaining, as both my hosts spoke perfect English. And then we were off again to Krlbo, Terry and Margaretta's home.

Margaretta was a good driver and conversationalist. "I don't want you to give the impression that Terry is now perfect and doesn't have problems, because he does," she said. "He still has fears, and sometimes he suddenly decides not to go on a campaign. Something inside him stops him, but I just make him go and he comes back full of joy because everything went so well and the Lord blessed his work."

We chatted away like old friends until, after nearly two hours' hard driving, I turned to Margaretta and asked if were far from her home. She said she would check the next signpost, and when we got to it, she was shocked to find we had been travelling 90 miles - in the wrong direction!

"I don't know what you must think of me," she said, turning a beetroot colour. "I was so interested in our conversation, I must have taken the wrong road."

She got out the map and soon we were heading back in the right direction. "Terry's going to ring me at home when he gets to a nearby railway station, and we can go and collect him. He wanted to get back tonight so he could see you."

I relaxed in Margaretta and Terry's neat, bright flat – the sort of little suburban home which represents the summit of ambition to most middle-class Swedes.

Margaretta prepared a cup of coffee to refresh us after our marathon journey.

"You will sleep just across the way in the wooden house my parents stay in," said Margaretta, handing me the steaming coffee. "They live close by so they can look after my baby Eve Marie-Louise when I am working and Terry is away."

Just then the phone rang and Margaretta answered and chattered in Swedish to her husband.

TERRY DENE: BRITAIN'S FIRST ROCK AND ROLL REBEL

She laughed merrily as she came back.

"He thought it was hilarious that I had taken you the wrong way," she said. "As soon as you're finished, we'll go and pick him up. It's about an hour's drive."

As we pulled into the railway station car park, Margaretta cut the engine and then went in search of Terry. Soon the couple, hand in hand, came bouncing back. Terry packed his guitar and suitcase in the back and insisted on driving.

"Great to see you again, brother," he grinned, shaking my hand. "I've had a great time at this place called Seffle. We've been in a coffee-bar and I've had lots of opportunities to witness face-to-face to kids. I've missed that, being up front, singing and preaching at campaigns. I think I ought to do more personal work . . . by the way, how are you, Dan?"

He talked enthusiastically about the effect of the campaign; he was like a kid who had just come top of the class. The journey soon went as Terry chattered away. "I really feel personal work is *the* most important work. After all, if someone hadn't been out doing personal work in Trafalgar Square that time, I wouldn't be a Christian today."

My head was in a whirl that night when I went to bed, and I still couldn't associate the excited young man I had seen, with the mean vicious pop idol of the past. Maybe Christ had made a big difference.

Next morning, Terry came over to my place and asked how I had slept. "By the way," he said casually, "there's a reporter and photographer from the *Daily Mail* coming over for a few days to do a feature on me. You don't mind do you? Great chance to witness to them."

Terry decided we should go for a drive and talk at the same time, so we gobbled down breakfast and went for a trip around the area. To start with, I had planned to interview Terry, note-book in hand, and was sure we would cover a lot of ground before the *Daily Mail* people arrived. But I soon found that Terry's mind works in short bursts, and I had to be content with any crumbs of information that fell my way.

"Let's not talk - let's just enjoy the scenery," he said. "My mind's tired and I don't want to overtax it. That's one thing I have to watch, getting too tired."

So we exchanged pleasantries during the short trip - I think Terry was really sizing me up - and we arrived back without me gaining much new information. He played me an LP made during a trip to England on the Pilgrim label, called "If That Isn't Love". Then he took out his photograph album. I thumbed through and noted it contained some pictures of him with Nemone Lethbridge at the premiere of *The Golden Disc*, others outside Wormwood Scrubs Prison with the Dene Aces after their trip "inside", and many of his time with Ken McCarthy.

"Have you any of your old hit records, Terry?" I asked, hoping to hear some of the songs I hadn't come across.

"Do you know, Dan, I haven't got one. I threw them all away after I became a Christian. I decided to turn my back on all that. I've had invitations to sing pop again, but I don't want any more to do with it.

"During the time I was a pop singer, I didn't think much about the words of the songs - the sound was the important thing. Now the words of gospel songs are everything because they contain the words of life."

That evening proved to be important - and fascinating. I was armed with a multitude of copies of cuttings kindly provided by the *News of the World* and the *Sunday People* libraries, and I wanted to see Terry's reaction to them.

So when Margaretta went to work at the nearby hospital, I spread them out on the kitchen table and asked Terry to look at them. He was quiet for a moment, and then slowly read through them. To my relief he laughed at many of them, saying: "Wasn't I a silly little kid? Just a silly rock 'n' roll singer."

But when we came to the Army cuttings, his face changed and I could see the incident still hurt him deeply. The public outcry and especially the remarks of some of the MPs afterwards had left a painful scar.

I quickly gathered the cuttings together and put them away. Terry made another cup of coffee and I said I would like to hear him sing some of his hits.

"I haven't sung them since I was converted," he said, taken aback. "Well, I suppose it won't do any harm. You'll need to know for your book, won't you?"

With that, he put down his cup, got out his guitar and began an amazing one-man show for me. I pictured I was in a frenzied, screaming audience at the Finsbury Park Empire during his heyday, and I had to concede that he could put over a rock song powerfully. For nearly an hour he forgot the embargo he had placed on his past, and gave me a top-of-the-bill performance, which ended with "A White Sport Coat" as Margaretta arrived back from work.

"Terry's just going over some of his old songs," I explained, as Margaretta looked suspiciously at us. "He's just sung 'A White Sport Coat'; have you heard it?"

Margaretta said she hadn't heard any of his hits.

With that, Terry sang the song for her.

"That's a very sad song," she reflected. "A very sad song."

*

Next day a minister friend arrived, and said he was going on a long drive to take his mother home and also to see his father's grave. Maybe we would like to join him?

We jumped at the invitation, and were soon on the road. The minister welcomed the chance to try out his English, and any words he got stuck with, Terry translated. I was impressed with Terry's Swedish. He jabbered confidently with the minister's mother and then turned to me to explain what he had been saying.

"I even pray in Swedish now," he said proudly. "I study a Swedish Bible and even think in Swedish. It was a long battle getting hold of the language, but I've done it."

We arrived at his friends' mother's home and trundled in, Terry clutching his guitar. Wherever Terry went, so did his precious guitar. Soon, he was tuning up, and singing for the mother and her sister, in a rather old-fashioned but pleasant living-room.

I watched with interest as his face lit up as he sang. The transformation was quite amazing. The care-lines seemed to disappear with the music. He sang several gospel songs, some in Swedish, and others in English, and then we sat down for a meal.

Later the minister took us to his "un-saved" sister's to say hello, and Terry again unpacked his guitar and sang for their family. Singing seemed more natural to him than talking.

Next day Margaretta was excited because we were going to Sveg, their wedding town, to collect Eve Marie-Louise from her parents, who had taken her for a few days' break while they coped with me.

The long drive to Sveg was not without its difficult moments, especially when a weary Terry curtly told me not to keep asking him questions. "I hope you're not expecting to get everything on this trip," he snapped.

I learned that Terry talks when he feels like it, and no amount of prompting from me or anyone else would elicit information. I also found out why he was in a bad mood. Singing his old hits had opened wounds, and in a delayed action sort of way he now felt very guilty at breaking the embargo.

But the black mood soon passed, and we were friends again. A smile spread over his face as he recounted a time in Norway when he was preaching, and his translator got a verse of scripture wrong.

"I was preaching about how hard I found it to witness. I said 'The Spirit is willing but the flesh is weak'. But the translation came out: 'The Spirit is willing but the meat is weak'. With that Terry roared with laughter, which woke Margaretta up in the back. "Sorry, love," he said. "I was just telling Dan ..."

"I heard ..."

As the endless pine forests slipped by, Terry confided: "I was born, really born, when I accepted Christ into my life. Before that I was in a prison of solitude. It was as if I was trapped in a lift between two floors. After my conversion, for the first time, I began to enjoy beauty. Do you know I often cry now when I see flowers. They are so beautiful. I never appreciated such things before.

"In the old days, the Terry Dene image gave me a false front, so I could act out a Jekyll and Hyde character. Everything felt so meaningless."

Terry stopped talking for a few minutes to get his thoughts together, and then went on: "I enjoy singing, I guess by now you've noticed that. There's nothing more exciting than praising God in song. I think it's great to be able to sing healthy songs. Don't get me wrong, I don't think all the songs of the world are basically evil - some are beautiful - but my reason now for not singing pop songs is that they do not give eternal life."

Soon we were discussing cockney humour, and Terry was at his most entertaining. He explained to his wife how "wide boy" comedian Arthur English told jokes. She smiled tolerantly as Terry mimicked Arthur English and I fell about laughing.

"Terry's a good mimic," she said. "That's why he has such a good Swedish accent."

The day got better as it went on, and when we arrived at Margaretta's parents' flat - above a police station - a piping hot meal was being prepared.

When the introductions were over, and after Terry had played with his blonde, cuddly daughter, he headed for the upright piano and began playing a fragment of symphony around the Genesis story.

Like Charlie Parker, all those years back in Hunter's Buildings, I was greatly moved.

"Like to see where we were married?" asked Terry as he replaced the piano lid. "It's only just over the road."

As we entered the beautiful church, Terry gave me an action replay of the wedding and said how nervous he felt.

"It was so different to the Edna affair," he said. "So different. There were no screaming kids for a start."

The journey back to Krlbo went well, and there were no sudden flare-ups. Next day the reporter and photographer from the *Daily Mail* were due to arrive and we went to the station to meet them. Jane Gaskell, the writer, and photographer Ted Blackbrow, were on time, and we went with them to their hotel to book in. Jane walked ahead with Terry, while I ambled along with Ted, who said he was glad to be away from London for a few days because of violence that had flared up over the docks situation.

"I've looked forward to this visit for a long time," he said. "I was a big fan of Terry's and always wanted to meet him in real life."

I wasn't sure how Terry would cope with the pair, or vice versa, but I soon found he was a "pro" in dealing with the Press. He had certainly had plenty of practice! But he not only wanted to give Jane Gaskell good "copy" - he wanted to convert her as well.

Whatever question she fired, Terry would bring his answer round to the Christian faith. He was involved in a "personal evangelism" situation and Jane listened to all he said, without arguing or provoking him. It gave Terry confidence, and he pressed on with enthusiasm.

He told Jane he had been under pressure from evil forces during his show-business days, and talked of "temptation" - but not in the way most psychologists and amateur psychologists talk nowadays, as though temptation comes from within. According to Terry, it really came from outside too. We are all at risk from strange forces, but can be helped by the supernatural too - forces of good, and chiefly Jesus Himself.

Terry told Jane he quite literally listens for the Word of God, and is satisfied he really hears it from time to time. All next day Jane fired her questions and Ted shot pictures from every conceivable angle. Then the following morning the pair decided to head back for Stockholm. But a "collect call" to London revealed that the powers that be wanted a picture of Terry talking to someone in the street, to contrast with the thousands of screaming fans he once sang for.

So Jane and Ted went on to Stockholm and Terry and I were to follow next day before I caught my plane home. Terry agreed to drive me to Stockholm and do the personal witness picture in one go.

I thanked Margaretta for her hospitality next morning, and told her I hoped Terry wouldn't drive 90 miles in the wrong direction! We arrived at Ted and Jane's hotel and chatted for an hour with them over coffee. Their plane was well before mine, so they had to get the picture and catch their airline bus.

Confident the picture wouldn't take long, Ted slung his camera over his shoulder and out we went, Terry clutching his guitar case. We headed for a likely looking square and hoped Terry would begin singing. But we found it was illegal to busk there, so we walked on. Surely, out of the mass of people, Terry would stop and talk to one? But he wouldn't. If the Lord didn't tell him to do it, he didn't, even if it meant that his visitors missed their flight. To Terry, this was a chance to win someone for Christ, not a publicity gimmick. We walked for at least an hour until we hit the Stockholm waterfront. By now Ted was nearly tearing his hair out, but Terry would not deviate from what he believed to be God's guidance.

It was just after we entered a small park near the docks that a shabby tramp stopped him and asked for money. This was the break. Terry got out some silver and handed it to the man, who guided him over to two other tramps sitting miserably on a bench. Ted began taking his pictures as Terry shook hands with them and then got out his guitar and gave the three tramps a private gospel concert and a short sermon – all in Swedish.

One of the men was in tears and told Terry he was a back-slider. Terry was convinced the Lord had guided him to them and spent 30 minutes talking and singing. It was a moving encounter. Finally he left them, and we set off to town. "Don't worry," Terry said. "I'll drive you all to the airport."

The journey to the airport was a joy, with Terry marvelling at the way God had guided him.

We all realised that here was someone who walked with the Lord, however falteringly.

I asked Jane for her impression of Terry. She told me: "Even when he takes his guitar and goes out into city streets and squares to 'testify', to 'witness' to the glory of his Lord, he will approach one person or group of people and not another – and he is listening all the time, for a sign to come through to him: who needed the Word in this street?

"This is true missionary discipline, and in fact he did say something about countries in Europe in the seventies needing missionaries as much as India and Africa did in the old days. It is fashionable to suppose that the place where Christian fervour is most necessary is the slum. But it is not escapism, as some of my friends suggested, that has taken Terry Dene away from his own part of London where it might be supposed he is needed most of all. It takes more guts, more sheer courage in many ways, to attempt to bring the hard and difficult laws of Christianity to a comfortable, materialistic society like Sweden, where nobody feels they really need anything, where even the cows in the fields look prosperous, chewing better cud than other cows get. Why should the clean, comfortable, well-fed Swedes put themselves out for salvation, when they reckon they've achieved it all right there?"

Jane described Terry's face as "something very touching to see". She added "The heavy eyelids, the wilful mouth, the moody jaw - they're all there, recognisable from the fifties photographs. But they seem all to have been honed out, purified. He has burned away the weakness he found in himself, like a surgeon coolly cauterising an unwanted wound. There's something there now that his Swedish wife and their daughter, and members of his congregation too, can lean on, go to for help and sense and a nice strong spiritual understanding."

Jane and Ted's flight was soon called and they went and Terry and I sat like a couple of old pals in the restaurant sipping coffee. "Tell the Christians back home that their prayers have not been in vain," he said as I was leaving.

Since my visit, Terry has made several successful trips to Britain, and now has settled here. He sang before 20,000 at Earls Court during SPRE-E '73, and many voted him the hit singer of the week. Terry has made many radio and television appearances and many old fans from the fifties have been in contact with me to say he is not forgotten.

Edna sums up her ex-husband like this: "Without his black moods, he was most endearing and very childlike. He could be cruel, but also had a great sense of humour."

She added: "I always believed he would be redeemed."

Terry Dene's story is not at an end. It's just beginning. He is only in his mid-thirties, but he has packed more into those years than most people do into a lifetime.

Terry Dene is no longer dead.

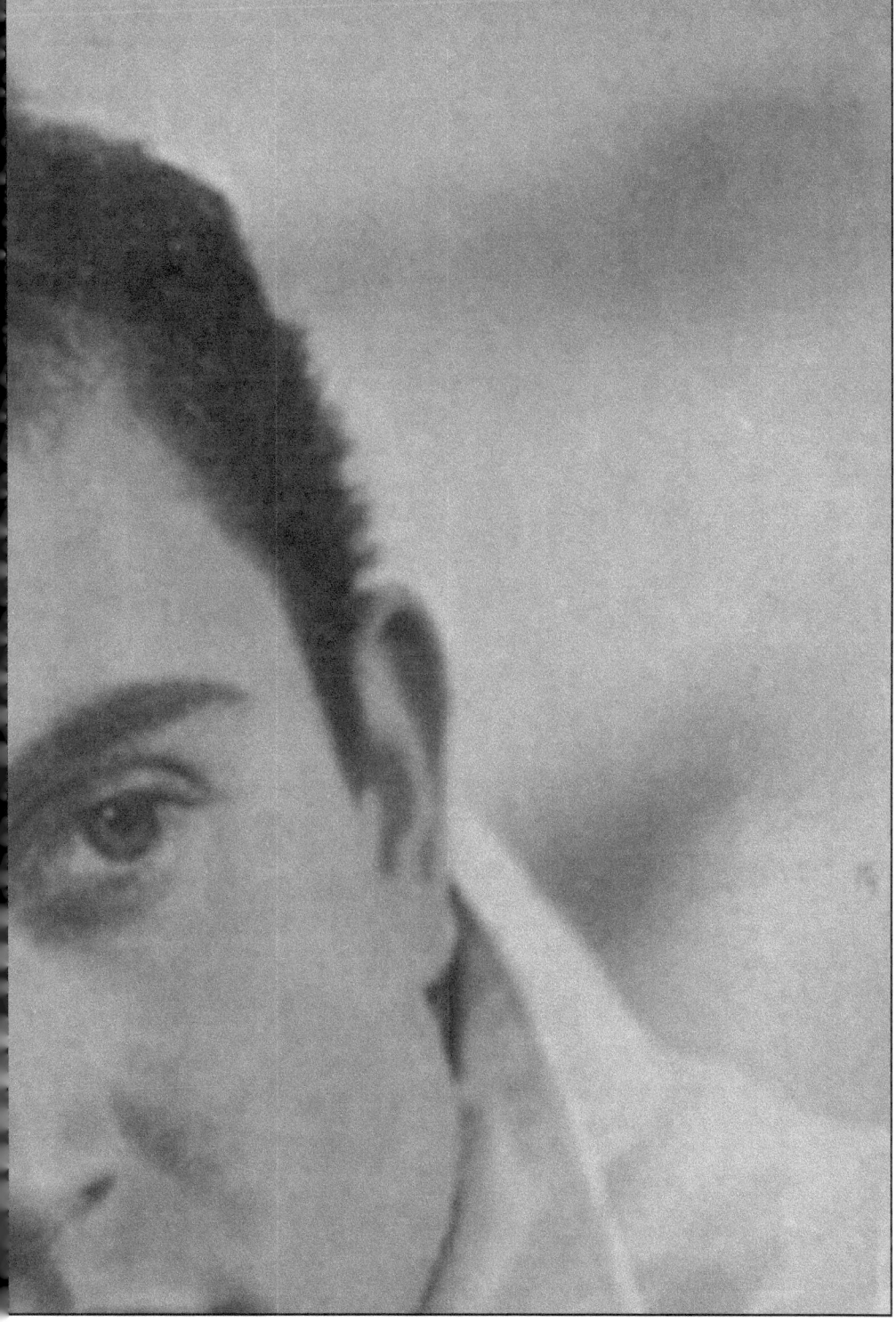

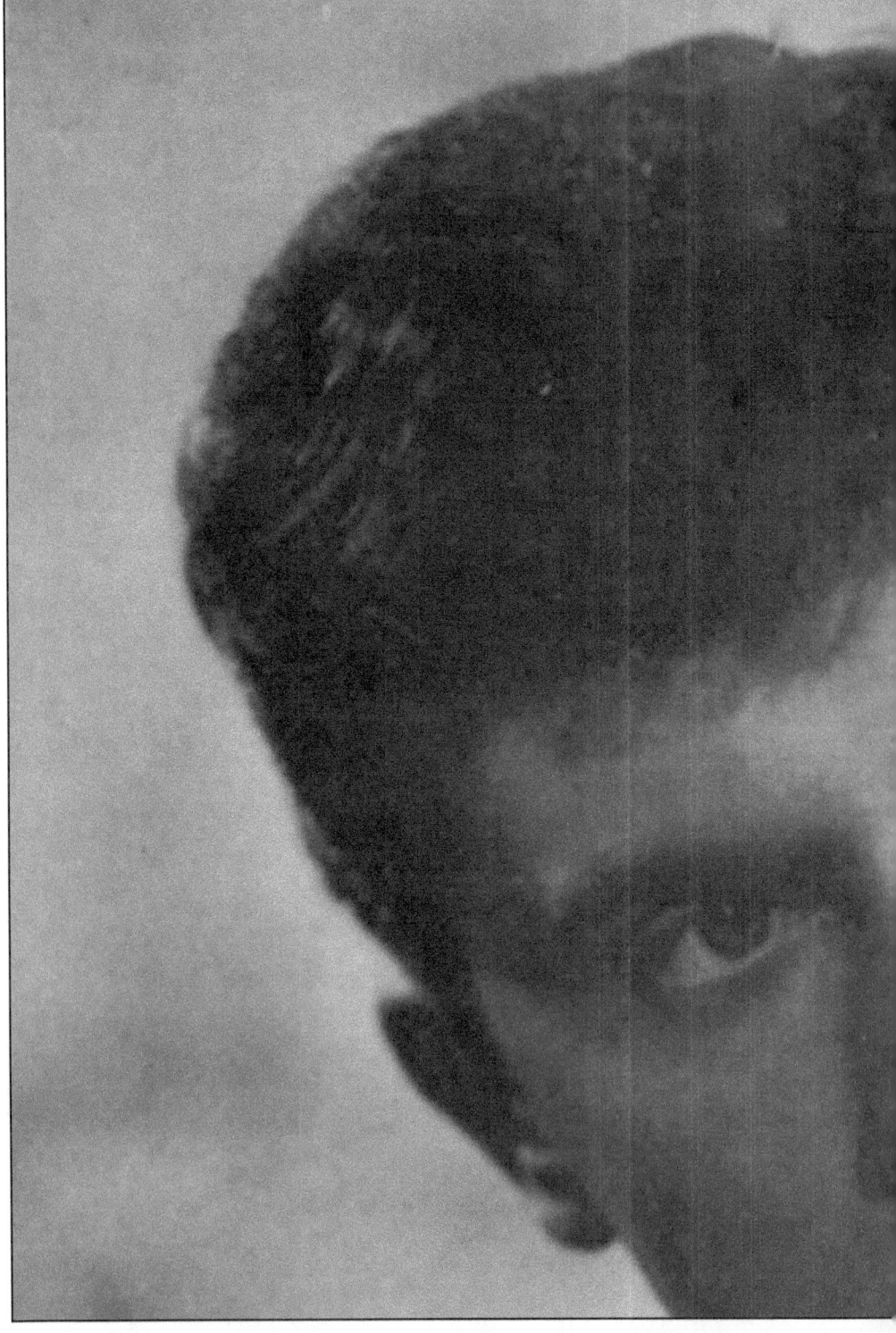

www.ingramcontent.com/pod-product-compliance
Lightning Source LLC
Chambersburg PA
CBHW070200100426
42743CB00013B/2987